on track...

The
Zombies

every album, every song

Emma Stott

sonicbondpublishing.com

Sonicbond Publishing Limited
www.sonicbondpublishing.co.uk
Email: info@sonicbondpublishing.co.uk

First Published in the United Kingdom 2023
First Published in the United States 2023

British Library Cataloguing in Publication Data:
A Catalogue record for this book is available from the British Library

Copyright Emma Stott 2023

ISBN 978-1-78952-297-6

Typeset in ITC Garamond Std & ITC Avant Garde Gothic
Printed and bound in England

Graphic design and typesetting: Full Moon Media

Follow us on social media:
Twitter: https://twitter.com/SonicbondP
Instagram: www.instagram.com/sonicbondpublishing_/
Facebook: www.facebook.com/SonicbondPublishing/

Linktree QR code:

...when I waked,
I cried to dream again.
William Shakespeare, *The Tempest*

on track ...
The Zombies

Contents

Introduction

Whilst there are few albums from the late sixties that I don't admire in some way or another, there are even fewer that I *distinctly* recall hearing for the first time. As that period yielded one of the finest musical harvests, most of what I heard was almost too much to really appreciate upon initial discovery. Yet some moments have pressed themselves whole like a dried flower into my memory. I know it was love at first hearing for the bucolic *Village Green Preservation Society*, but I couldn't tell you exactly when and how this love-struck, much the same for *The Piper At The Gates Of Dawn*, *Are You Experienced*, *Ogden's Nut Gone Flake* ... Yet, the exact moment I heard The Zombies' *Odessey And Oracle* has remained with me, not only as a musical epiphany but also as a moment of sheer serenity. It was summer, the weather was bright and hopeful, there was promise in the air. And something had changed by the time the record finished ...

It would have been enough if The Zombies only ever achieved the profound beauty of that album; creating at least two classic singles before it, and continuing to be both a live and recording act of both power and imagination, sweetens their afterlife even more.

The Zombies

In another life, The Zombies might have gone on to be bankers, art lecturers, English teachers, and anthropologists, or at least if you believe their early publicity. Much ado was made of their (supposedly) prodigious number of O Levels and promised, but deferred, university places. However, winning The Herts Beat Competition in May of 1964 changed this completely; not only had The Zombies garnered an impressive local reputation and a dedicated following, they'd won £250 and a recording contract. They were now just six months away from an American number one ...

At least two of The Zombies came from musical backgrounds: keyboardist Rod Argent's father had led The Les Argent Quartet and then Les Argent and his Rhythm Kings; meanwhile, Ted, the uncle of bassist Chris White, was a renowned saxophonist and composer, and White's dad Harold had also played double bass in swing bands. It might not be surprising then that Argent and White would go on to be the chief songwriters for the band, although White was the last to join.

Rodney Terence Argent was born on 14 June 1945 to Les and Molly in St. Albans, Hertfordshire. Molly was one of eight children, providing Argent with a large extended family that would also prove to be helpful in his career because cousin and bassist Jim Rodford was a vital influence and champion – he'd also go on to be a latter-day Zombie. It was at Rodford's house that Argent heard Elvis Presley, sparking an interest in rock 'n' roll that would last a lifetime. Argent described it as 'two and a half minutes of music that changed my life'. He first learnt the harmonica at around the age of seven before moving on to the piano, and although he took formal lessons as a child, his passion first fired when, by ear, he managed to work out 'Swinging Shepherd Blues' by the Canadian saxophonist Moe Koffman, discovering how to harmonise around triads in the process. Not only did Argent have a grounding in rock 'n' roll and jazz, but classical music also struck a loud chord. Being taught music by Peter Hurford (who would later be made an OBE in honour of a very distinguished career as an organist and composer) introduced him to another world and, in particular, Bach. Hurford organised a performance of Bach's oratorio *St Matthew Passion* with St. Albans choir in which Argent was a chorister. He said it made him think, 'This is what music's all about'. When putting this alongside the other types of music that had fed his creativity, he remarked, 'It all felt like music from the same well'.

The oldest Zombie, Christopher Taylor White, was born two years previous to Argent on 7 March 1943 in Barnet, and later attended St Albans County Grammar School, where he met vocalist Colin Blunstone. Colin Edward Michael Blunstone arrived only ten days after Argent on 24 June 1945 in Hatfield. Coincidentally, his father Arthur was an engineer at the de Havilland factory, an aviation manufacturer where Argent's dad also worked, although it is thought that the seniors Blunstone and Argent didn't know each other.

But there was another link to the factory: drummer Hugh Birch Grundy (6 March 1945, Hampshire – making him the only Zombie not born in Hertfordshire) was a classmate of Argent's at St Albans School, and he'd moved to the county when his father Ted (an amateur violinist who made Grundy's first drum kit) got a job as an aircraft inspector at de Havilland's. Argent and Grundy wouldn't become mates until Argent began to think of getting a band together. However, it would be 1961 before this began to take shape; after Argent saw Grundy drumming in the school band, he asked if he'd like to create a group with him. Argent had already approached Paul Atkinson (Paul Ashley Warren Atkinson, born 19 March 1946, Cuffley) through the school folk club after being struck by his guitar playing. Atkinson's initial instrument had been the violin, which he eventually swapped for a cheap guitar – much to his mother's chagrin. As it happened, Atkinson and Grundy had already played together for a while. Meanwhile, through mutual friends, Argent had been helping another County Grammar School boy and neighbour, Paul Arnold, to build a bass guitar in Atkinson's dad's wood shop. Not only did Arnold join the band on bass, but he informed them that his mate Colin Blunstone was seeking a group too. Blunstone was told to meet the lads outside The Blacksmith Arms, and whilst his first musical impression must have been a strong one (Blunstone recalled performing Ricky Nelson's 'It's Late'), the personal impression he made was quite different. He told Robin Platts of *Goldmine* ('Time of the Zombies', 14 April 1995):

I remember when we first met that Saturday morning, I had a badly broken nose and two black eyes. My nose was all taped across – and I think I looked pretty aggressive – because they didn't know me at all. I played a lot of rugby when I was at school, and I had broken my nose, and I think they thought I was fairly rough and tough.

And then there were five.

At first, Argent intended to be the lead vocalist of what he initially envisaged as a guitar band, one of which Blunstone was playing. An early piece they performed together was the sultry 'Malaguena' by Ernesto Lecuona, whose dramatic peaks would go on to influence Argent's initial compositions. However, it is a classical guitar piece and suggests a very different sound to the one that came to characterise The Zombies. As they had little equipment at this time, Jim Rodford stepped in to lend them drums and offer pointers for getting started, including some drumming tips for Grundy. Argent said: 'Hugh had never played kick drums in his life. He picked it up really quickly'.

Rodford would later confess that he had little faith in the band at first and refused an invitation to join! He told *Times Series* in 2014 of his rationale: 'I was in the biggest band in the area, so why would I want to play with some young kids?' It wasn't long, however, before the band dynamic shifted for the better; after Blunstone heard Argent playing B Bumble and the Stingers' reworking of Tchaikovsky's 'Nutcracker', cleverly named 'Nut Rocker', he advised him to play keyboards instead. Blunstone has also said that he couldn't master The Shadows' 'Wonderful Land', leading him to re-think his musicianship. Luckily, when Argent heard Blunstone singing some Ricky Nelson songs, he was deeply impressed by his voice, and their destined roles were suddenly obvious. Their first gig at Lemsford Village Hall went well enough to prove this change was worthwhile. There was one hitch, however: the band questioned Arnold's commitment. Argent told *Mojo*'s Johnny Black in 1997 that his own keyboard playing would often result in bleeding hands:

I'd put on an Elastoplast, but it would seep through, so I'd keep adding more. It was quite spectacular, all this blood on the keyboard. So I was going crazy, and the others were jumping around, but I looked over at Paul one night during 'Peggy Sue', and he was just standing there with his left hand in his pocket. He'd figured how to play the bassline on open strings, and, as the hall was chilly, he put his free hand in his pocket. Clearly, his heart wasn't in it, so we fired him.

It wasn't long before Arnold departed to follow a career in medicine, eventually practising in Canada. Nevertheless, he'd not only ensured that the band had a distinctive and superb singer in Blunstone, but (for the time) he'd also given them their obscure moniker. Whilst not everyone was an admirer of the band's name (members of Manfred Mann urged them to change it), it was certainly preferable to the erstwhile The Mustangs, The Sound Albans or even The Sundowners, taken from the 1960 Robert Mitchum film. Although, I do have a fondness for one of their other incarnations: Lady Chatterley and the Gamekeepers. Not averse to taking inspiration from literature, one wonders what a concept album by this line-up might have sounded like, especially after 'the end of the Chatterley ban and the Beatles' first LP…' In 2014, *Music Times* listed The Zombies in their run-down of bands who sound nothing like their name. Yet, the idea of resurrection, a driving determination and a haunting legacy are certainly apposite. In the liner notes to *New World* (an album recorded in one of their many after-lives), the band say they had decided to split *even before* taking part in the Herts battle of the bands, but their victory in the prestigious contest saved them. A pattern of extreme success followed by inexplicable failure would dog their short but fruitful tenure.

The first rebirth of the band came when Arnold was replaced by Chris White. However, Terry Arnold, Paul's brother, remained as their manager for the time being. Argent had already met White a few years back, but White didn't recall this. Argent told me in 2023:

> Chris was a wonderfully musical person … Before we formed the Zombies, there was a knock on my parent's door one day, and Chris White was standing outside. I'd never met him in my life. He said, 'I hear you play piano'. I don't know where he'd heard this because I played nowhere except my front room, and he said, 'Would you like to be in my dance band?'

Argent turned him down and didn't think he'd ever see him again and was very surprised when White walked into their rehearsal. White not only brought his bass skills to the band but also an unusual and semi-public place to rehearse: above his dad's shop. The space was so cramped that they decided to use the roof for one session, drawing a large crowd! Things moved quickly after White joined, with more regular gigs and a burgeoning local following. However, White himself initially cut an enigmatic figure as he wasn't actually introduced to the rest of the band properly until about a month later. Nevertheless, their playing went from strength to strength. Grundy told *Goldmine*:

> We got such a following that, eventually, so many people used to want to come down there when we were playing; they had to hire a marquee and erect it alongside the clubhouse so they could get more people in. By the end of the evening, the walls would be awash with sweat, and the floor would be awash with beer. They were tremendous evenings. I think it was that which gave us the confidence and inspiration to enter the Herts Beat competition.

By February 1964, they had played their first non-local gig in Kings Langley and Kinston Upon Thames. They'd also performed at Ballito's, where Argent met the guitarist and pianist from the Laurie J Combo, Vic Briggs, who'd go on to play with Steampacket and, later, Eric Burdon's Animals. Briggs suggested incorporating 9th and 13th chords into Argent's playing, which successfully shifted the band's sound away from the simpler RnB covers that dominated their setlist towards something more jazz-orientated. Argent explained to me in a 2023 interview:

> He was so sweet. After our set, he said, 'I really love what you were doing in 'Summertime', your soloing, but have you ever thought of this?' If you were soloing on a minor 7th chord, imagine a 7th chord a 4th below it and play a scale that fits with E minor, and suddenly, the things that had been driving me mad when I heard early Miles Davies, I was hearing those intervals! It was such a lovely thing for him to do.

Soon, even better gigs followed, so much so that Argent was able to buy a Hohner electric piano, a pianet, which he'd first seen and heard being used by Manfred Mann. This would mean he would now always be in tune and would always be properly heard! Argent told *Goldmine*:

> When you depressed a note – on the end of a mechanism was a little rubber suction pad with sticky stuff on it, and this attached to the note, which then bent up until the sticky pad could hold it no longer, and it sort of broke away from it and went 'boing'. It was made by Hohner. It was their first electric piano. There were all sorts of problems with it because the sticky stuff on the pads used to attract hairs and make buzzing sounds and things because of that. I used to have to dry it with a hair dryer because any moisture used to make crackles and things, so it was very primitive, but it was a great sound.

Come May, they were competition winners. Patrick Stoddart was a young journalist, reporting for *The Watford Observer*, who had written an article entitled 'Is There a Watford Sound?' It opened portentously: 'It was not long ago that when darkness fell over Watford, the population took to its homes and television sets searching for something to break the monotony'. The article went on to explore how the sound of Hertfordshire encompassed beat bands, folk singers and jazz players. As the article was written right at the start of 1964, this puts the county ahead of the charts, as a blend of these sounds would soon proliferate. But the week this went to press, the Top 20 housed The Swinging Blue Jeans, The Dave Clark Five and Freddie and the Dreamers, indicating that the charts were less varied in sound than that of the Home Counties, in turn, highlighting the distinctiveness of The Zombies' unique debut 'She's Not There'. I asked Argent and Blunstone if they remembered a characteristic folky sound in the area: Blunstone recalled how Donovan had played during the interval of one of their gigs at Welling Gardens. Argent added: 'Maddie Prior [later of Steeleye Span] used to come along to our gigs. She used to get up and sing 'Summertime' with us'.

However, not only did Stoaddart's article celebrate the local scene, but it also sparked a way for it to be trumpeted more loudly and broadly. Consequently, *The London Evening News* sponsored a battle of the bands, setting up a £250 prize fund and getting the backing of Watford Council.

But the bands had to work for it! The Herts Beat contest lasted over two months as groups won different heats, competing on Sunday evenings. By the time of the final, The Zombies' setlist consisted of mostly cover versions, including 'I'm Going Home', 'Summertime' and 'I Got My Mojo Working', but also boasted their first self-penned number, Argent's 'It's Alright With Me.' The judges were Shane Fenton from The Fentones, who'd later be more successful as Alvin Stardust, and Sandra Barry, whose backing band was an early formation of The Action and whose record label was Decca – the company who offered to sign The Zombies as a result of the competition. Although, some sources say the band was approached even *before* they'd been declared victors. *The Watford Observer* reported on their triumph: 'After the results had been announced, it took half an hour to clear the stage so that the photographers could see the groups – and in that time, The Zombies must have signed their autographs more times than ever before in one day'.

As well as the exciting opportunities this win would bestow, the band had not only beaten runners-up The Beat Six but another of the most popular bands in Hertfordshire – Jim Rodford's own The Bluetones, who hadn't actually made it into the final at all. A year back, it would have been unthinkable that Argent would beat his cousin and mentor, so progress was fast. Anyway, no matter for Rodford, who would join The Mike Cotton Sound as a bassist before taking his place in Argent, Rod's eponymous group after The Zombies, in 1969.

The Zombies' triumph also drew fleeting interest from Philips, but the band struck up a strong deal on the advice of producer Ken Jones, whose company Marquis would take the group on as an independent act and then lease them back to Decca. This meant that the songwriters would at least get a fair slice of royalties in the future. Grundy expanded to *Goldmine*: '...we've been with Marquis ever since. The music is still with them and they are the ones who do these wonderful deals for us, the compilation albums that come out and all sorts of different things, which is why we receive royalties now'.

Following the contest, they were due to enter the studio; they at least had a little more experience of this than of business contracts, having previously recorded some demos, including the standard 'Summertime', a few months ago. This track, a lifelong favourite of Argent's, would influence their first hit and their last ...

Yet, despite technical proficiency, inventive songwriting and a vocalist whose throat sounds like it's made of silk, The Zombies would only spend *ten weeks* in the UK Top 40. Quite rightly, this is seen as one of the great injustices in pop music.

But no matter: The Zombies' songbook is superb. Let's begin here.

The Early Singles (June 1964 – January 1965)

> O, wonder!
> How many goodly creatures are there here!
> How beauteous mankind is! O brave new world,
> That has such people in't!
> William Shakespeare, *The Tempest*

It's probable that The Zombies' comparatively early feats cost them long-term triumphs. Having only just begun to write songs, they had no reserve to draw on when they went into the studio and were under pressure to compose and record hits in quick succession. Their limited experience of playing live as professionals on the gig circuit also meant that, even though their publishing deal was sound, their management deal would be knottier. Tito Burns replaced Terry Arnold, but Arnold remained as a road manager, much to Blunstone's displeasure, as, for reasons unknown, the two didn't get along. However, in hindsight, Burns should have been more of a cause for contention. Nathan Burns had been an accordionist, playing with various groups and acquiring his nickname Tito – meaning little one. He had then led bands such as the Tito Burns Sextet, which included Ronnie Scott and John Dankworth. A flavour of Burns' management style is evident in a clip from the Bob Dylan documentary *Don't Look Back*, in which Burns, along with Dylan's manager Albert Grossman, set the BBC and Granada against each other in a battle for the star. Whilst Burns would secure the band's tours in the US and Europe, his methods were questionable: he sold the band to an agency managed by his wife, thereby effectively making him their promoter and agent – an illegal position and one which would greatly disadvantage the band financially.

Whilst not exactly an overnight success, the move to being recording artists was a sharp shift. Atkinson explained to *Goldmine*:

> I had to get the afternoon off school. I had to take a note from my mother to school to be excused at mid-day. And all my friends at school thought it was great. They couldn't believe it – Atkinson's got the afternoon off because he has to make a record!

It also meant there was little time to contemplate the band's image. To The Zombies' annoyance, a marketing ploy was to bill them as the posh eggheads of the pop world. Even in the notes that accompany the reissue of Argent's first two albums in 2000, John Tobler was still describing the band as middle class and as having all attended the same prestigious school. In truth, their backgrounds were relatively modest, with Argent growing up in a council house and winning a scholarship to St Albans Grammar School. He continued to *Goldmine*:

13

It was crazy! Because of the juxtaposition of the name Zombies, which means 'brain dead' in a way, and the fact that we had quite a few O levels and A levels between us, they thought this was a good story. And once the story came out, journalists, who are often very lazy, just look back and pick up the same thread again and again. It was something that used to really annoy me because it was a stupid focus.

Peter Jones, writing for *Record Mirror* on 22 August 1964, titled his article 'The Zombies: The group with the brainpower' and wrongly labelled them 'ex-university lads'. Even in a 2023 interview with me, Blunstone was loth to talk about how the band had been perceived. He explained:

> I'm reluctant to say that one of the reasons that we struggled in the '60s was that a very false image was created for us. The trouble is if you discuss it, it re-energises it... There was a very short conversation (at Decca) that limited the kind of success we could have in the next few years.. They said, 'New band, what have you been doing?' And the answer was, we hadn't been doing much, we'd only just left school. As we often say, Paul Jones was at Oxford! And there we were labelled as academic geeks – your career's over, mate. They want you to be pirates and brigands, not the class swot.

Argent added: 'We were very badly managed, and so he didn't make any attempt to change that'.

Their supposed academia was emphasised by publicity shots taken by David Wedgebury, which show the group staring grimly at the camera and with White and Atkinson wearing thick, dark glasses, lending them a Harry Palmer quality. In reality, these photographs have been unfairly singled out because images of The Who and The Stones, by the same photographer at the same time, also have a static feel that belies the legendary excitement of the bands *now* but would have seemed standard for the time. Wedgebury elaborated to Johnny Black:

> I did several photo sessions with them, but compared to other people I photographed, like the Stones, Bowie or Bolan, who were all intensely image-conscious, The Zombies lacked identity. Two of them wore serious-looking glasses, and they all dressed in the same suits, which contributed to this scholarly image. They didn't do themselves any favours.

Manfred Mann's early shots have a similar quality (but The Zombies are always keen to point out that some of them are actual graduates), and it seems that the same problem that befell The Zombies' music – essentially either being slightly ahead or behind the times at various points – also affected their image: the identical suits had been a successful marketing gimmick for many, yet, it was beginning to fade out by this time. Blunstone is right that the record company didn't seem to put much thought into how they could support such an inexperienced band. But, poor image or not, it didn't impact on how their first single would be received.

In terms of following the band track by track, it is a bit of a bugger. They're in the unusual position of having nearly a two-year gap between their first two albums. However, during this time, they released many singles, sometimes duplicating either an A or B side – this has made it a challenge to trace. However, it's part of The Zombies' story that an excess of singles were released in this way, and so I have outlined these in the order they came out, even if they appear on a later album. It can also help us to see songs in a new light when considering them alongside the company they're released in. Therefore, there are times when I also think about them as album tracks.

She's Not There b/w **You Make Me Feel Good**

Personnel:
Colin Blunstone: lead vocals
Rod Argent: electric piano, backing vocals
Chris White: bass, backing vocals
Paul Atkinson: guitar
Hugh Grundy: drums
Recorded at Decca Studios, London, 12 June 1964
Producer: Marquis Enterprises (Ken Jones)
UK Release: 24 July 1964
US Release: 3 October 1964
Chart placings: UK: 12, US: 1 (Cashbox), 2 (Billboard)

'She's Not There' (Rod Argent)

Well, let me tell you 'bout the first time I heard this song, or, to be exact, a mere morsel of it. You might recall those awful compilation albums that joined bits of re-recorded 1960s hits together on one side of vinyl as a 'mega-mix'. I must have been about ten when I found an unloved one in our record collection at home. It wasn't the sort of thing my parents would buy, and the fact it was lacking a cover and looked like a cat had tap-danced on it, probably meant it had been left behind after a party. However, as by this time, I was determined to hear every single piece of music from that hallowed decade, I played it anyway. In between what was possibly 'Rubber Ball' and 'The Night Has A Thousand Eyes', was just a snippet of 'She's Not There'. It was new. It was sinister. It was stunning. But sadly, a few years would pass before I discovered it was The Zombies.

It sounded unique then, and still does; how did Argent, who had written only two songs previously, achieve it? (It's often described as his second composition, but he'd written 'The Lonely One', inspired by 'Please Please Me', for The Bluetones first before 'It's Alright With Me'). The initial impetus was from producer Ken Jones, as he'd advised the band to write more original material, and whilst the rest of the group didn't seize this chance, Argent and White certainly did. Argent decided to listen to some music before composing, and whilst not being of *musical* inspiration as such, John Lee Hooker's 'No One Told Me' ignited the lyric – although Hooker's track also contains an almost tearful piano line that must have been appealing to the keyboardist too. Fittingly, 'No One Told Me' was the working title of 'She's Not There' and the phrase helps to direct the lyrics so that they not only lament the absence of a woman but also assert a feeling of betrayal from friends who didn't warn of *La Belle Dame Sans Merci*. There's the contrast between what the singer wasn't told and his now demanding 'Let me tell you 'bout...', almost as if he's angrier with his friends than his lover, creating an intriguing unease that is sharply matched by the music. Argent told me: 'I wanted to construct a story'. This narrative is supported extremely well by the tension in the melody and arrangement.

Argent added a potent pop word to the mix: '*Well*, no one told me...' John Lennon remarked how exciting this word is in the lexicon of rock 'n' roll, referencing 'Be Bop A Lula', and Lennon himself would thrillingly use 'Wellll!' to open his visceral 'Meat City', a blistering track on the otherwise bland *Mind Games*. The Zombies would revisit this trope and would continue to confide in their listener in a number of songs. But there is another potential inspiration in terms of the ethereal presence in (or not in) the song. Nicholas Pegg, in his consummate *The Complete David Bowie*, noted a similarity between 'The Man Who Sold The World' and the poem 'Antigonish', aka 'I Met A Man Who Wasn't There', by the American writer William Hughes Mearns. Written in 1899, it was supposedly prompted by a true haunting in Nova Scotia.

Yesterday, upon the stair,
I met a man who wasn't there
He wasn't there again today
I wish, I wish he'd go away...

It was adapted into a song by Harold Adamson and Bernie Hanighen, 'The Little Man Who Wasn't There', and was recorded by Glen Miller, with Tex Beneke on vocals, and then there was a later version by Bing Crosby. In common musically with 'She's Not There' is the jittery rhythm and its minor chord foundation. Another curious twist is how the second stanza details looking around the hall for the missing figure, an almost film noir-ish detail which would be echoed in 'Gotta Get A Hold of Myself' by Dee Dee Warwick and covered by The Zombies themselves.

The musical inspiration is broader, however. Whilst the atmosphere and key of 'Summertime' are echoed, this track is actually in the Dorian mode, something that Argent felt was kindled by Miles Davies' 'Milestones', which uses both the Aeolian mode and Dorian mode to create a slight, but conversely sorrowful hopefulness across the piece. Jazz musician Pat Metheny pointed out to Argent how 'She's Not There' is also a modal piece, with Argent, at first, doubting this observation. It obviously owes a debt to the minor chords of 'Summertime', but is a little higher, creating a tone of surprise but also one of sincerity, as evident in the narrator's spooky and sorry tale. The term Dorian evolved from the ancient Greek people, the Dorians, who were noted for their honesty and strength, making the singer's confession all the more poignant and potent. Whilst it took a while before the truth of Metheny's comments struck, Argent was aware of the importance of the minor/major shift as he was composing.

In the liner notes to the 2008 reissue of *Odessey And Oracle*, Chris Welch recounts that Argent was fascinated by the striking shift from a minor to a major chord in Clint Ballard's 'You're No Good'. Originally, this was recorded by Dee Dee Warwick in 1963, but it also became a Top Three hit for The Swinging Blue Jeans a year later, just as The Zombies were winning the Herts Beat contest. Incidentally, The Blue Jeans recorded the song on the advice of the drummer's girlfriend, Sue Johnston, who went on to join *The Royle Family*. Both versions of 'You're No Good' have similar dynamics to 'She's Not There' with a surging chorus and a slinking bossa nova beat. There were several hits, both in the UK and the US, making use of the bossa nova at this time, from the vibrant 'Viva Las Vegas' by Elvis Presley to the wistful 'The Girl From Ipanema' – 'She's Not There' manages to blend both of these. Writing in *Changing Times: Music And Politics In 1964*, Steve Millward makes the convincing argument that 1964 was a miraculous year for 45s and traces the rise of bossa nova in pop from Bacharach and David's 'Always Something There To Remind Me' and 'Walk On By'. Millward also notes how Chris Andrews's 'Girl Don't Come' is in a similar fashion. Despite the beat being part of the Brazilian samba, a dance of celebration (it has to be noted that samba does arise from the music of black slaves, so its meaning is complex and shouldn't be over-simplified), these songwriters use it almost ironically. Bacharach had been influenced by the *Getz/Gilberto* album from March 1964 by Stan Getz and Joao Gilberto, which featured the pioneer of bossa nova beats, drummer Milton Banana, which also included Astrid Gilberto's version of 'The Girl From Ipanema'. Although 'She's Not There' was certainly distinctive, the audience had been readied for it in some way because of these hits.

However, another source for the minor shift has been cited by Argent: 'Sealed With A Kiss' (written by Peter Udell and Gary Geld), originally released by The Four Voices in 1960 and a hit two years on for Brian Hyland, who'd play Dick Clark's *Caravan Of Stars* in 1965 a few months after The Zombies had. In the form of a letter, it recounts how the singer is missing his lover, lamenting absence again and employs a chord shift similar to The Zombies, creating an oscillation between hope and despair. Geld said he took his inspiration from the German composer Bach, making it obvious

17

why Argent, a lover of classical music, would admire the piece. Later, Argent would also use the conceit of a letter in a love song, but in a very different context, for 'Care of Cell 44'! Argent remarked to Alec Palao in the liner notes of *Zombie Heaven*:

> I'd always thought of the verse of 'She's Not There' to be mainly Am to D. But what I'd done, quite unconsciously, was write this little modal sequence incorporating those chord changes. There was an additional harmonic influence in that song. In the second section, it goes from D to D minor, and the bass is on the thirds, F# and F, a little device I'd first heard in 'Sealed With A Kiss' and it really attracted me, that chord change with bass notes not on the roots. And I'm sure I was showing off in the solo as much as I could!

However, the track opens with an understated keyboard line, punctuated by the sibilance of Grundy's drums before Blunstone's confessional, whispered vocal. From their earliest hit, The Zombies established a cohesive style, consistently playing in a way that complements the entire band. Whilst the drums dominate the rhythm section, the bass and the especially sparing guitar, which were recorded on the same track, never compete for attention. The cool verses are skilfully balanced with the controlled hysteria of the chorus as Blunstone's voice climbs, yet it still doesn't break the soughing tone. This then repeats with Blunstone breaking out on the second chorus, building the tension before the relief of the electric piano solo, a scribbling counterpoint to the vocalist desperately keeping his cool. The Hohner pianet was a judicious choice, as the Vox used on the live Saturday Club performance (available on *Zombie Heaven*) is just too thick and too *present* on the delicate verses. The track repeats the first part of the song before it climaxes with an emphatic blast of the chorus; in just over two minutes, the band have created a vignette of despair that transcends mere teenage angst.

Chris White also credited producer Jones with developing the track, telling *Mojo*'s Johnny Black: 'When Rod played 'She's Not There' to Ken, it was shorter, with a longer piano break, and Ken suggested going back to the verse again'. It is perfectly structured, creating a compelling mood. Indeed, the song's atmosphere was still being evoked on later 1960s recordings, as on The Doors' 'Light My Fire'. In fact, The Zombies' influence on The Doors, in general, is often underexplored, but Jim Morrison's croon to rock yelp is excellently done here by Blunstone. The Zombies also set in motion another of their recurring ideas: the enigma of being unable to articulate through language, whilst a sonically flawless recreation of frustration is possible.

However, a song of such skill and discipline had a chaotic birth. Terry Johnson was to be the chief engineer for their first recording session, in which they would lay down this song. Gus Dudgeon, who was the assistant, got his big break instead. His illustrious career saw him go on to work with David Bowie (being one of the laughing gnomes, no less!), Elton John and The Beach Boys, and he is also believed to be the first person to have used sampling when he produced John Kongos on 'He's Gonna Step On You Again'. However, for now, he was the novice, yet ended up replacing a drunkenly truculent Johnson, who was ignominiously carried out of the session by the band holding a limb each. Things reached fever point when they were attempting 'You Make Me Feel Good', and Johnson began effing and jeffing at the band's intonation of the backing vocals. Feeling disappointed with their experience so far, The Zombies then began to work on 'She's Not There'.

The story fragments here because there are several versions of what might have happened. We have to give thanks to Claes Johansen for the thorough account in the essential biography *Hung Up On A Dream* from 2006, who explains how the mono version of the song was crafted (this is the only version of the song, in my opinion, as the stereo lacks the distinguished rhythm because of how it needed to be mixed) and notes that it had some extra beats added after the recording was over. Whilst Blunstone's vocals were recorded on the first take, Argent said that Grundy struggled with the rhythm and so the snare was added later to accentuate a sense of uncanniness. Argent has also revealed that the way in which Ringo Starr broke up rhythms influenced the drumming, too. Now, some believe that the overdubbed drums were the work of Terry Johnson, who had previously been a drummer and might have felt that, instinctively, this was what the track needed; others feel he had something to make amends for, as he had cocked up the first recording session of a hotly tipped new signing. Johansen observed that tom toms and cymbals are present on the mono also, meaning that Johnson's contribution might even be more significant than this.

Yet, in the equally thorough *Time Of The Season: The Zombies Collector's Guide* (1999) by Greg Russo, Jones is said to have recorded the drum overdubs himself, whilst yet another version has members of the band requesting the overdub! Whatever the origins of the beats, their omission from the stereo version is a painful loss, and Argent still winces when hearing the 'wrong' version played on the radio. This was corrected to some degree when Grundy overdubbed the stereo recording, which was released on *The Zombies Decca Stereo Anthology*. The drums almost stagger, imbuing a feeling of exhaustion but still a dogged determination to warn others, that fit the lyrics cleverly. Argent has said that the rhythm was part of its composition. Blunstone added: 'When Rod writes a song, most of the arrangement comes with it'. Therefore, however, the rhythm was enhanced, it had originated with Argent.

Now that the track had been recorded, it was time for the band to consider what was to become of it. White had also written 'You Make Me Feel Good' as a response to Jones's advice, and the group debated if this or 'She's Not There' would be the A-side, but it is hard to believe that any other track would have been seriously considered. Blunstone commented: 'There was an incredible energy when we played it. I do remember being really excited about that song'. Full of hooks, from the piano line to the syncopation to Blunstone's superb vocals, it was surely impossible for it not to succeed. Yet, success was of an initially modest kind, at least in the UK. Released in July 1964, it was September before it peaked at number 12, and was likely given a shove by George Harrison, who wholeheartedly voted it a hit on *Jukebox Jury* when he appeared on the panel alongside Alexandro Bastedo, Carole Ann Ford and Reg Varney (Blunstone and Burns would appear on the show themselves in January of 1966). Argent was particularly delighted by Harrison singling out the talent of the keyboardist, feeling rightly proud, and Harrison would go on record as being impressed by later Zombies releases, too.

As the band conquered the Top 20, they were sandwiched between Elvis Presley's' 'What A Night' at 13 and Cilla Black's underrated ballad 'It's For You' at 11, which was written by Lennon-McCartney. The era-defining 'You Really Got Me' was number one, and pop was teetering on the edge of rock. Within a few months of turning professional, The Zombies were credibly competing with past and present giants, and it seemed that future conquests were a surety. By the end of the year, 'She's Not There' was at the top of the *Cashbox* chart in the US and only just kept off the *Billboard* top spot by one of the many interminable early 1960s Bobbies – Bobby Vinton with 'Mr. Lonely'. Talking of the *Cashbox* chart, this was only the second song performed and penned by a UK band to reach number one after 'I Want To Hold Your Hand'. Like the UK at the time, America had more than one chart, which can make this challenging to discern. *Cashbox* was the chart of a music magazine akin to *NME*; the other chart was *Billboard*, which calculated sales from reports by radio stations and record shops, so the two charts didn't always tally. Nevertheless, The Zombies were now a mighty force in the British Invasion – UK acts dominating the US charts, spearheaded by Acker Bilk's 'Stranger On The Shore' topping the US charts in 1961 and then The Tornados' 'Telstar' in 1962, before The Beatles' take-over at the end of 1963.

Whilst the track might have had the most success across the pond, for a song about absence, it's remained present in the pop universe in many guises across the globe. The first was The Jaybirds (who'd transform into Ten Years After) in 1964, with a faithful version, but with more prominence given to the rhythm guitar. Next were the Swedish band Ola & The Janglers in 1965: theirs is a musically sound rendition, but the vocal is almost a parody of Blunstone, if a cute one. The Janglers also recorded a song entitled 'No, No, No' that just might have taken a pinch of inspiration from 'Tell Her No'. The Knickerbockers knocked out a strong take, also in 1965, and added some tasteful brass that works surprisingly well; UK Subs successfully blended garage and punk in their short but punchy cut from 1979; Tim Curry's interpretation in 1981 owes a debt to David Bowie; Crowded House's unexpectedly dull attempt appeared on the soundtrack of the Russell Crowe film *The Crossing* in 2000, whilst Christopher Cross's 2014 version is a by-numbers smooth ballad that lacks any drama. At the last count, there are 145 takes on the song.

The best-known covers, though, are probably Vanilla Fudge's typically overblown attempt from their eponymous debut album in 1967. It's one of their least successful takes as the real star of the track is the melody and the rhythm, and using it as a vehicle for virtuosity doesn't work (although the melodrama would inspire Neil MacArthur's single – more about this later). This also besets the most famous version by Santana, although Argent cites it as his favourite. It was Bill Graham's suggestion that Santana find a place for it on 1977's *Moonflower*, but it stamps down too hard on the snaking melody. Nick Cave and Neko Case recorded it for the soundtrack of the vampire saga *Trueblood*, turning this monologue of despair into a murder ballad duet with groans of accordion in the arrangement. Even The Zombies have covered it in their private lives! After their split, some members, including Blunstone, performed it at Argent's wedding along with 'Summertime' in 1972. However, an unexpected interpretation of the song came from a most unlikely source: The BBC's *One Show*. The programme filmed an interview with Argent and Blunstone, taking the audience through The Zombies' career and culminating in the St. Alban's choir's acapella performance in the cathedral where Argent used to sing as a boy. However, I could have done without the cringe Crimewatch-style reconstruction of their first recording session, which dramatises their encounter with pissed-up engineer Terry Johnson ...

Not only has there been a multitude of covers, but it has an illustrious number of admirers, and even Elvis Presley is said to have it on his jukebox. The Zombies were told that Presley was a fan by his uncle (some sources, including Argent, think it was Presley's father Vernon, rather than his uncle) when they made an unexpected pilgrimage to Graceland – alas, the King himself was away filming.

However, the presence of 'She's Not There' would be in abeyance in the wake of the 11 September attacks, as it found itself on the banned list of songs because its content was deemed potentially offensive.

'You Make Me Feel Good' (Chris White)

The B-side to 'She's Not There', and also White's first composition to be presented to the group, 'You Make Me Feel Good' was a band favourite that Grundy said he would have liked to re-record later in their career. It's an uncomplicatedly catchy song with the lyrics concisely summed up in the title, and sonically, it recalls The Beatles' 'You Can't Do That'. Although White is the composer, Argent advised the shift to a sharp major to increase the excitement. The laconic piano intro is wonderfully casual, before a dry guitar sound and a restrained riff, actually written by Argent, is revealed, and it is well complemented by the keyboards. Mostly recorded live, there was again some overdubbing of the drums.

Whilst this is a much less original sound than the celebrated A-Side, it evinces how the band could be at once current and far-seeing on the same release: in theory, a perfect pairing that should have put the group in good stead. John Mendelsohn, reviewing the cheapo collection *The Zombies: Early Days* in 1969, wrote, not completely damningly: 'a slightly laughable Peppermint Lounge-type twister complete with idiotic "oh yeah's"'.
However, it's Metal Mike Saunders who sums it up best: 'It's a knockout, the most preposterous sex song I've ever heard – it sounds like an eight-year-old eunuch singing! Great'.

The Buckinghams recorded it as 'You Make Me Feel So Good' in 1966, speeding it up and including an unsuccessful 'spontaneous' guitar solo.

Leave Me Be b/w Woman
Personnel:
Colin Blunstone: lead vocals
Rod Argent: keyboards, backing vocals
Chris White: bass
Paul Atkinson: lead guitar
Hugh Grundy: drums
Recorded at Decca Studios London, 31 August and 5 September 1964
Producer: Ken Jones
UK Release Date: 16 October 1964 (UK only single)
Chart placing: UK: did not chart

'Leave Me Be' (Chris White)
Unloved by the band, Argent went as far as describing it as 'a terrible single… limp and weak' to the *Bob Lefsetz Podcast*, and he believes its failure set the band on their long decline from US number one to the non-charting wilderness. It also began the band's frustration with Jones's production, as he'd tried to make the song sound like The Righteous Brothers' 'You've Lost That Loving Feeling'. This went against what White had requested, which had been more like 'You Make Me Feel Good', just as the band had performed it live. However, whilst the demo does have a slightly harder edge, certainly in the drumming, it's not that different from the official cut.

Blunstone described it to me as 'a disastrous second single. But it was the only song we had. We didn't think it was commercial. We didn't want it as a single. In America, they skipped that single. There was a lot of short-sightedness in the industry at that time. They thought in terms of a three-year career cycle'. But is the track as wretched as its reputation?

Quite simply, it's too much of a rehash of the cool but simmering tension on 'She's Not There' to be an unqualified triumph. As a song considered by itself, it's excellent. Opening with some mournful guitar strums and then 'If it seems that I'm too quiet', the guitar echoes Blunstone's whispered vocal, a cause of disagreement, as the band didn't want to re-use this technique.

In the liner notes of *Zombie Heaven*, Gus Dudgeon said that Jones, not unreasonably, saw Blunstone's voice as The Zombies' 'gimmick' and wanted to spotlight it on their follow-up. The band were so displeased that the vocal was re-recorded, but this version wasn't released as the single in the UK. It's not quite a carbon copy of 'She's Not There' as Blunstone's tones on the chorus are bluesier, and the guitar solo is less jazzy with more of a hint of a jagged garage sound. The affecting lyric is haunting too, with 'Love just cannot end at parting; my world's dropped from under me'. It's the hangover after the drama of 'She's Not There', and something of its melodic melancholy must surely have influenced early Graham Gouldman. And despite some of Argent's misgivings regarding Jones' production, he also commented to Lefsetz that Jones was the master of creating an echoing quality on Blunstone's voice, bestowing a trademark despondency to their work and ensuring a uniqueness that is on full display here.

'Leave Me Be' might also have made a better closing track on their debut album *Begin Here*, which it wasn't included on. Instead, 'Got My Mojo Working' filled this position in the tradition of rockier numbers closing albums, such as The Beatles doing 'Twist And Shout', 'Money' and 'Dizzy Miss Lizzie'. However, as 'She's Not There' closed the A-side, this would have lent a pleasing symmetry if it had been the climax of the album. Maybe it would be a more loved track too …

Sandie Shaw reviewed the single for *Melody Maker* and, despite it being a 'blind test', was able to identify it immediately as The Zombies, which probably sums up the blessing/curse nature of this track. The band had a sound but felt it was a compromise, and already, they were beginning to think about how they might produce themselves, especially when the song didn't chart, except in Australia. Blunstone told Will Simpson from *Classic Rock* in 2008: 'With the benefit of hindsight, we needed to wait. Rod had only just started writing, so we didn't have a back catalogue of songs to choose from. None of us felt very enthusiastic about 'Leave Me Be'.

Yet, the song was admired by some, with the loyal Ola And The Janglers recording it, as well as The Posies. The irritating, overstated vocal on Sonny and Cher's interpretation shows the good taste of The Zombies' version, whatever their opinion of it.

Perhaps the composer wasn't so fond of it, as White nearly got into trouble because of the song. An avid fan of this track followed him from Norway to the UK, confessing her devotion to the writer upon arrival. White turned her down and thought no more about it until a Salvation Army volunteer came hunting for her on behalf of her frantic parents. Allegedly, she'd already moved on to The Rolling Stones' Brian Jones…

'Woman' (Rod Argent)
An up-tempo track that, if unremarkable, demonstrates a different facet of the band's sound. Opening with a walking guitar riff and displaying a

controlled but fizzing keyboard solo from Argent, which is undoubtedly the track's highlight, it is more a promise of what was to come than a delivery. However, the jejune aspects of the song are apparent in the title being sung across too many bars and also in the wavering vocal from Argent, who performs this as more of a duet with Blunstone. The verses are stronger, showing that Blunstone and Argent's voices were able to cohere well, and this is particularly borne out by the demo version available on *Zombie Heaven*, which lacks this and, therefore, much of the track's appeal. The demo reveals a similar arrangement but also includes a middle section, which is repeated twice and merely drags it down; a country and western feel is at odds with a straight-up bit of rhythm and blues.

The track is enhanced by some more drum overdubs, possibly by Terry Johnson again. However, it does show how propulsive the bass is on this track and shifts the attention to White's musicianship as well as his songwriting.

The lyrics cover some well-known territory, with an indecisive singer who feels something will happen with the wonderful woman, though he just 'can't concede' this. Despite it being the slightest of The Zombies' output so far, it was again covered by other acts, with the Swedish band The Mascots revisiting it in an irritatingly messy cut in 1966 and The Buckle sticking more with The Zombies' blueprint in 1967.

Tell Her No b/w Leave Me Be (US release) and Tell Her No b/w What More Can I Do (UK release)

Personnel:
Colin Blunstone: lead vocals
Rod Argent: organ
Chris White: bass
Paul Atkinson: guitar
Hugh Grundy: drums
Recorded: Decca Studios London, 25 November 1964
Producer: Ken Jones
UK Release Date: 29 January 1965
US Release Date: 2 January 1965
Chart Placings: UK: 42, US: 6

'Tell Her No' (Rod Argent)
Inspired by Burt Bacharach's use of 7th and 11th chords, which Argent described as 'jazz colourations', he wrote the aching middle eight first – it's such a pristine pop song, that it had to be hit. At least it was in the US, going Top Ten, but the UK didn't allow it to get into the Top 40 – philistines. However, Argent could content himself when Little Anthony from The Imperials told him how much he admired the song. Argent explained to me about its composition:

We'd just been on tour with The Isley Brothers and Dionne Warwick. And Dionne Warwick did a lot of Burt Bacharach songs. And Burt was using major 7th, 9th, 11th and even 13th chords sometimes, and I thought, I want a bit of that as well. I was self-taught and finding things out for myself ... I think there might even be a B13 in there.

Something of a legend now for its use of 63 'no's in the chorus, this song is the anti-'She Loves You', with a friend advising a mate to stay away from a girl. In fact, it's the advice that the singer of 'She's Not There' laments not receiving. Beginning with 'And', which Greg Russo noted was unusual for a pop song, but would also be used by Chris White on Argent's 'Hold Your Head Up', it creates an *in medias res* effect which suggests that this conversation has been going on for some time, justifying the unequivocal, 'No, no, no!' Another winning detail is the exhausted mumbling in the second verse, which might seem like design but was really because Blunstone had recently woken from napping as the backing track was laid down: it must only have been a catnap, as take four secured it. Nevertheless, the sleepy singer wasn't alert enough to recall the lyrics, yet no one seemed to notice. That this escaped everyone's attention is a testament to how somnolent vocals were now an established Zombies trait. Blunstone appears to be singing, 'Don't hurt me now from your arms', which makes more sense than many pop lyrics anyway...

Opening with a stuttering guitar riff, later to be reflected in the chorus, the verse moves from major to minor chords, dashing the hopes set up by the conditionals of the girl's potential attention. Blunstone's rueful tones work well, not a self-parody as might be implied regarding its contentious use on 'Leave Me Be', and there's a gorgeous glow to the harmonies that's matched by a gleaming tone from the keyboards, with some real power in the bass adding to the speaker's determination. Just as the chorus risks losing its compulsion, the middle eight swings in, this time moving from the minor to a major 7, lending the piece a romantic sweep. Grundy's drumming is a highlight too, with the easy swing of the verse contrasting with the staccato of the chorus; the frustrated rumbling fill into that bittersweet middle eight is a particularly clever detail. Atkinson is elemental too, with Martin Sharp of *Perfect Sound Forever* noting that 'he uses acoustic guitar to perfection; his playing on this song is both tender and tough'.

In his article '5 Reasons the Zombies Should Be in the Hall of Fame' from 2016, Michael Gallucci writes: 'It's a great song, barely two minutes long, but not a second is wasted. And at around the 40-second mark, singer Colin Blunstone lets out a sensual but vulnerable "whoa-oh-oh-oh" that ranks as one of popular music's all-time greatest wordless asides'. It's undoubtedly one of Blunstone's most balanced performances, between the yearning and the proselytising, making his long-lasting but comparatively modest career as much of a puzzle as The Zombies' struggle as a whole.

Like all Zombies' singles, it was rapidly covered with The Five Emprees first to the post, then The Mummies having a go, who must be given extra credit for using their band name almost as a cover version too! Del Shannon gave it a country edge in 1975 and Juice Newton's 1983 version is also in the country style. It has to be said that all pale when compared to The Zombies' version, which is a masterclass in pop songwriting, performance and arrangement.

'What More Can I Do' (Chris White)
One minute and 35 seconds of superbly iterated frustration that many punk bands would envy, this is short but bitter! Whilst Metal Mike Saunders was absurdly tin-eared regarding *Odessey And Oracle*, he did comment insightfully in his 1972 article for *Fusion* – 'The Zombies – Everything You Wanted to Know!' He writes: 'In their own way, this group express the same sentiments of disorientation, confusion and communication breakdown as eloquently as Black Sabbath has with 'Paranoid''. The singer, as once again succinctly captured in the title, is running out of options as he tries to trust his love.

An almost-ascending riff begins the track, but it soon falls back down again, a neat metaphor for the exasperated lyrics. The song is peppered with some great defiant fills from Grundy and the drums have an ear-catching dry sound that holds the attention. This is further enhanced by a spiky guitar solo, made more effective by a lack of sustain on the notes. The organ has an almost clanging tone on the solo, emphasising its percussive element. There is much-considered detail here for what is almost a snippet of a song. Admittedly, the vocal is a little lost in places and, at times, Blunstone seems to be mimicking more of Argent's tone. However, even though Argent's voice is thinner and less mature at this point, we can see why Blunstone does this for this youthful track. The aggravated stutter of drums that closes it works really well, too.

A first-class live version for *Saturday Club,* with the Vox organ enhancing the mounting pressure and an angrier guitar solo, graces the *Zombie Heaven* boxset.

The Zombies EP
Personnel:
Colin Blunstone: lead vocals
Rod Argent: organ
Chris White: bass
Paul Atkinson: guitar
Hugh Grundy: drums
Recorded: Decca Studios London, 12 June – 5 September 1964
Producer: Ken Jones
Release Date: 29 January 1965
Chart placings: UK: did not chart

Although recorded between summer and autumn previously, this was scheduled for later release as The Zombies took their place on a package tour in the US. They did appear twice on the UK show *Ready Steady Go,* once in September and then again near Christmas, but Christmas itself was spent in the US.

They closed 1964 with performances in Murray The K's Christmas shows and the band's education in showmanship and the American sound went beyond music. Another American sound was that of gunshots, which they heard from their Brooklyn hotel each night. This climaxed in Grundy and White, along with The Nashville Teens, witnessing a man being shot dead. White told Johnny Black: 'That was the big shock, blood all over the pavement and the police coming along and picking up spent cartridges. And it never even appeared in the papers'.

Nevertheless, 1965 began auspiciously: the band made their US TV debut playing 'She's Not There' and 'Tell Her No' on *Hullabaloo*, introduced by Brian Epstein. The band gave a typically cool and arch performance, despite the presence of a *Hullabaloo* dancer draped on a chaise longue (look out for Argent's nonplussed reaction to the plaster bust of the classical composer beside him). Yet when it gets to Argent's solo, the director (usually Steven Binder, who worked with Elvis on the *Comeback Special*) cuts to the drummer for its entirety! Argent continued in a 2023 interview with this author: 'When it got to the solo, they were totally confused. They just went to the drums. Solos were guitar things, then. [Later] they wanted us to dance with people from *Westside Story*!' Blunstone carried on the story: 'They realised it was a challenge, one step beyond us! Years later, I did take dance classes. But after about six months, I had to give up as I was injuring people!' This half-baffled response to the band would foreshadow how later Zombies singles would be met, too. Yet playing on one of the most watched music programmes in America might have indicated that the band's next release could not fail on either side of the Atlantic, but their fortunes took a dip within a few weeks as the EP bombed and didn't chart in the UK.

EPs were always a harder sell, being more expensive than singles; there's also the issue of which tracks would get picked up for radio play when each side offered more than one track, so its lack of success is not inexplicable. At the time, it might have seemed a safer bet to display their eclectic sound, but despite there being many pleasing moments, there is no one track the equal of 'She's Not There', and, inadvertently, Decca was suggesting that the band's eventual LP might not quite hit the mark by keeping its release back. However, despite it arguably being the least explored of The Zombies' releases, it's an important chapter in the development of their sound and a satisfying listen for the most part.

'Kind Of Girl' (Rod Argent)
The band felt more could be done with this track, and alas, it is let down a little by a lumbering middle section, which doesn't suit the smoothly rueful verses. Yet, the drum fills leading up to this part increase a kind of

petulance inherent in the lyrics: the singer appears to have been betrayed by yet another friend, as well as his lover. Another (sort of) ascending intro and outro make this an apt lead track for the EP as the final note leads into the gorgeous acapella opening of 'Sometimes'. The diminished chords that flash as the lyrics tell of a better girl twist the tension and are evidence of a maturity in the writing beyond Argent's years. The demo available on *Zombie Heaven* has a slightly faster intro and the lyrics are a little different. Furthermore, the middle section is lively and the organ trills leading into the guitar solo should have been retained. Interestingly, the organ on that version is heavier too, foreshadowing their later sound.

'Sometimes' (Rod Argent)

It might be a stretch to say that the title of 'Summertime' ignited this track, yet there's a harmonic warmth to the intro that also recalls Gershwin's piece. The lyrics tell of how the singer's lover soothes his loneliness in the night, which matches the lullaby of 'Summertime' too. After the serene opening, it breaks into a standard RnB cut that's given light by some Beatles-esque harmonies and the switch to a wistful bridge. The economical but effective guitar solo shows that Atkinson's playing was never a flashy distraction but was almost always *exactly* what the track needed. In some ways, Atkinson's work is underappreciated and out of the many great guitarists of the 1960s, his name is often neglected. Argent said to me: 'Paul Atkinson was the first guy I asked to be in the band because I saw him at a school in a folk club. In a corner, Paul was playing and I thought what a lovely sound he was making... He had a bit of magic playing in this club'. Blunstone referred to an unnamed later guitarist who couldn't resist improvising around the songs. He said: 'It makes it quite challenging for the guitarist as we've always been a keyboard-based band. It's probably as important what the guitarist *doesn't* play'. Atkinson's work fits this perfectly.

Zombie Heaven includes a snippet of the band practising the intro, with Blunstone being asked to demonstrate his style to the others. Jones gets the band to re-do it because he can 'hear a smile' that shouldn't be there.

As the penultimate track on the first side of the US version of *Begin Here*, which was simply titled *The Zombies*, it gets a little lost, especially as it's then followed by 'Woman', which has a similar tempo and atmosphere.

'It's Alright With Me' (Rod Argent)

Originally recorded in The Zombies' first studio session (before their battle of the band's victory), this spirited track could have been an A-side. Although 'Summertime' (that track again!) seems an unlikely inspiration for this song, it was demoed at the same time as the standard and the organ solo has a shimmer of its melody, which is also echoed in the closing refrain. An arresting element of the song is the slowed-down middle eight, emphasising its jazz origins. Not only does this song introduce how important the ambience and structure of 'Summertime' was to be to The Zombies' sound, but it also establishes another motif: the descending intro, here lending a frisson of excitement to what is a surprisingly chilly lyric.

Whilst the title appears optimistic and relaxed, this isn't completely the case. The working title was the dour 'Hole In My Bucket', which is alluded to in the second line, 'got a leak in my bucket and a great big hole in my floor...' The song goes on to list all of the narrator's failings, but he's at least willing to accept someone else's opinion of him. Yet, there's the curious 'So you see I can only offer a man that's poor/With frost in bed...' hinting that his shortcomings are not merely materialistic. This is in contrast to the many bragging and macho pop songs of the time, with the image of him lacking 'a big black car' not being the subtlest Freudian hint! This song makes it obvious that The Zombies could knock out a solid R&B track but still add something of the originality of 'She's Not There'. Also, Blunstone's vocal is stronger and more controlled on their original numbers rather than the covers, and his considerable skill is evident here as he's singing live with the band.

Claes Johansen writes:

> Considering the youth and inexperience of its writer, certain features here are quite advanced, such as the way that the main chord sequence is imitated between each stanza in the form of a guitar riff. Equally interesting is the bridge where a Bb chord is dissolved into a G – a slightly unusual harmonic shift of a kind that can be found in many other Zombies songs throughout their career.

Overall, the track shows a mastery of shifting rhythms and is a burst of energy akin to The Swinging Blue Jeans' take on 'Hippy Hippy Shake'. The fizzing half organ, half guitar solo template that the band would return to is also laid down here.

The track can also be found on the first side of *The Zombies*, where it effectively breaks the reverie that lingers after 'Summertime'.

'Summertime' (George Gershwin, Ira Gershwin, Du Bose Heyward, Dorothy Heyward)

It was Chris White's idea for the band to cover this standard and it would prove to be a pervasive and long-lasting influence on their career from their early singles (it informs the scale of 'She Not There', of course) through to 'Time Of The Season'. When I saw the reformed band in 2005, they closed their set with it, explaining their fondness for the track before apologising for playing it on a rainy night in Manchester! It was indeed the first song recorded by the band as a demo and was reworked after their battle of the bands victory, (although not dramatically) being a contender for their debut single. Patrick Stoddart, a journalist for *The Watford Observer* at the time of The Zombies' local triumph, told Johnny Black when he heard them perform this at the contest: 'When they did 'Summertime', I remember thinking that Colin was comparable with the best blues interpreters'.

However, it was Chris White who'd performed it before any of the other Zombies: he'd played with an acoustic trio before joining the band and they'd arranged the standard with a waltz beat.

Billie Holiday had been the first to take the track into the US pop charts in 1936. George and his elder brother Ira wrote the music for the play *Porgy* (1927), which had been penned by the Heywards and was based upon Du Bose's novel from 1925. Set in South Carolina, it tells of the disabled black beggar Porgy and his love for Bess, who's involved with a violent drug dealer, Crown. However, 'Summertime' is sung by Clara, a fisherman's wife, to her baby as a lullaby. This makes it perfect for Blunstone, whose vocals have a dreamy and somnambulant air. It's often said that his style is 'breathy', but this is a partial and somewhat cursory description of a sensuous, gentle, but clearly potent tone. Furthermore, the 'breathy' quality was also played up by Jones, who would use compression to emphasise it. A more exact analogy can be found in 'Blunstone's melodic, crystalline, aching voice, resembling a dry wind' from Harold Bronson, *Phonograph Record*, in 1972, describing a tender muscularity. Another beautiful depiction is from Eric Harvey, writing for *Pitchfork* in 2020, explaining the 'downy tenor' of Blunstone's voice. In this track, the warmth and sleepiness are enhanced by his pronouncing 'fish' as 'fizz': 'The fizz are jumpin…'

White and Argent had admired Miles Davis's version from 1959, but whereas his is light and airy, there's a pleasing darkness to The Zombies' interpretation, more redolent of late summer evenings with a hint of autumn in the air. Blunstone's phrasing is perfect, indeed better than Sam Cooke's curiously uncertain delivery in his 1957 version or Al Martino's dogmatic intonation from 1960. That Blunstone could outdo such accomplished vocalists so early in his career proves what a remarkable frontman he was. But the rest of the band aren't overshadowed at all: it's clear they had a talent for arranging, as they'd worked most of this out prior to being in the studio. The song announces itself with three gentle chords, like a slow stroll, before the bass joins like the parents of the lyrics coming together. Another pleasing moment is how Argent's dancing solo begins before Blunstone has finished his line, imbuing a gorgeous fluidity. However, sadly, like all good summers, the song is too short! It was cut with a longer solo, but this was removed, presumably to keep it chart-friendly. Perhaps a compromise could have been adding a second solo rather than one long one. Regardless, it shows a prodigious talent as The Zombies' take is original, despite so many versions already existing, and they give it something of their own character as Ricky Nelson's 1962 cut did, with its distinctive riff being recycled by Deep Purple for 'Black Night'. Admittedly, The Zombies' version has some of the smokiness of The Chris Columbo Quintet's 1963 release, but the keyboards are certainly more tasteful!

Returning to the demo, which they'd recorded in April at the Jackson Brothers Studio a few months before, it's a very similar arrangement and it's understandable how it would impress both Ken Jones and the Herts Beat judges. Admittedly, the waltz is overstated, lending it a jerky, slightly mechanical quality, but the band clearly ease into it, as the final take attests.

She's Coming Home b/w I Must Move

Personnel:
Colin Blunstone: lead vocals
Rod Argent: organ
Chris White: bass
Paul Atkinson: guitar
Hugh Grundy: drums
Recorded: Decca Studios London, 2 March 1965
Producer: Ken Jones
UK Release Date: 9 April 1965
US Release Date: 27 March 1965
Chart Placings: UK: did not chart, US: 48 (Cashbox) 58 (Billboard)

'She's Coming Home' (Rod Argent)

Given the working title 'I Cry No More' by Argent, this was inspired by Herbert Howells' 'Magnificat And None Nunc Dimitris' from 1946. Howell was a composer of organ music, but his daughter Ursula is probably more famous, having played roles in Amicus horror films and the sitcom *Father, Dear Father*. The piece translates as Magnify/Now Let You Depart and Argent admired it from his choirboy days, feeling it had a bluesy quality. Ironically, his take on it would recount the arrival of his love as opposed to a departure.

The production has a Phil Spector vibe caused by the sonorous drums and the reverb on the vocal. It opens with Ronettes-type beats before Blunstone's luxuriously rich vocal takes over. The use of sharp minors in the uncertain verse is a crisp contrast to the triumphant majors of the more assured chorus. However, the shifting rhythms here don't work as well, with a jumpy lead into the bridge and then an abrupt middle eight – it's a lot to take in for a single. Each segment is interesting by itself, but it's easy to see how this could evade an audience as it doesn't catch the ear on a casual listen. The lessening of the drums' power as the song reaches its climax is a curious decision, too.

It's a bit of a patchwork of mid-60s acts, with not only Spector but also The Walker Brothers being evoked. This demonstrates that the band could step into any style with little difficulty, but in trying to escape 'She's Not There', it's possible that their identity was being adulterated, making single sales difficult. Nevertheless, it reached 21 in Canada and like every Zombies release, if the UK or US wasn't listening, the wider world often was.

'I Must Move' (Chris White)

This is an interesting new sound from White, beginning with a sweet, folky melody that shifts to a chorus fattened by a hint of Indian drone and just a shiver of The Kinks' compelling 'See My Friends'. Both White and Grundy, in particular, were admirers of The Kinks.

As is evident once more from yet another apposite title, the singer regrets that he cannot stay in the relationship but must keep on the run instead. Whilst not the most original of lyrical premises, the fragile arrangement compensates: the shift to a 7th chord lends a sense of uncertainty as Blunstone sings, 'And I can't stand still'.

This was initially titled 'I Believe in You' and had a different lyric, but the revised one corresponds to the melody better.

Begin Here/The Zombies (US Release)

Personnel:
Colin Blunstone: lead vocals, guitar, tambourine
Rod Argent: keyboards, lead vocal on 'I Got My Mojo Working', backing vocals, harmonica on 'Work 'n' Play' and 'I Got My Mojo Working'
Chris White: bass, backing vocals
Paul Atkinson: guitar
Hugh Grundy: drums
Ken Jones: piano on 'Work 'n' Play', tambourine on 'I Remember When I Loved Her'
Recorded: Decca Studios London, 12 June – 12 December 1964
Producer: Ken Jones
UK Release Date: 9 April 1965
US Release Date: January 1965
Chart placings: UK: did not chart, US: 39

Tracklisting for The Zombies:
Side One:
She's Not There
Summertime
It's Alright With Me
You've Really Got a Hold on Me/ Bring It on Home to Me
Sometimes
Woman

Side Two:
Tell Her No
I Don't Want to Know
Work 'n' Play
Can't Nobody Love You
What More Can I Do
I Got My Mojo Working

The Zombies' debut album *Begin Here* has much in common with *With The Beatles*: there are superb originals but also a surfeit of superfluous cover versions, yet they do have a qualified charm. The album is often seen as a let-down after the promise of their debut single, but this needs to be examined in context. In recent years, most people have been introduced to the band through the sublime *Odessey And Oracle*; consequently, it's difficult for other work to stand alongside it.

However, as a debut, it's varied, polished and often comparable to other works of the time. But, this is where it gets thorny: it was released in 1965 but is an album of 1964. Mark Deming for *AllMusic.com* retrospectively said:

It's still a fine album and certainly better than what most of their peers had to offer in 1965, but what could have been an achievement on a par with The Kinks' *Face To Face* or the Beatles' *Rubber Soul* ended up being something quite good instead of an unqualified triumph.

This ignores how the songs were actually written and recorded in 1964, and when heard alongside *Beatles For Sale* or The Kinks' eponymous debut also from that year, it's not of an inferior quality. Argent explained to me that he saw it more as a document of their live act and that the album's title was decided by him and White as a kind of introduction to the band.

Returning to the similarities with The Beatles' second album, the cover portrait is photographed similarly, with a close headshot on two levels of the group not smiling, but instead of black and white, there's an effective rose-violet wash by Czechoslovakian photographer Dezo Hoffman. This seems to indicate how things had already shifted, but The Zombies' music was a little behind. And even a few weeks in pop is a gulf.

Blunstone revealed to *Record Collector* in 2008:

It was recorded extremely quickly. There was a lot of pressure from the record company to record an album very fast. We were recording probably four tracks every evening; it had to be mixed, and the artwork sorted out very fast. There are many good songs on the album, but I wish we had a little more time. The other problem was that before 'She's Not There', we were an amateur band, so we were doing lots of covers like Beatles tunes and standards. We needed songs we could put our identity on, and songs had to be written very quickly. Even the covers we played were found just before the studio time came up, so it was a bit of a rush.

He elaborated on this to me in 2023: 'Decca wanted a single from us every six weeks. We were touring constantly. And it's very hard to write and record when you're touring all the time ... We just didn't have the repertoire to record an album. Material-wise, it was quite challenging'.

The album was recorded in the evenings over a few weeks and the sudden success of 'She's Not There' demanded that the band move fast. Using a four-track recorder meant that the lead vocal would take one of these, the backing vocals another, the supporting instruments on one together and then a lead instrument would be given the final track. Eventually, the band, including Blunstone, would be frustrated by how his vocals would always be foregrounded by Jones, who believed this to be The Zombies' unique selling point.

Despite the album having a number of highlights, the reviews also mostly focused on the strengths of the lead singer. Peter Jones in *Record Mirror* wrote: 'Average instrumental and vocal work, but the lead vocalist has a very distinctive voice which could be the asset to keep this decent group near the top'. Sharpening the sting all the more, in the same edition of *Record Mirror*, there's an advert for 'She's Coming Home' using the dreaded sleeveless pullover shots, again showing how the image of The Zombies was out of step with their music and how they'd leapt forward in both songwriting and arrangement by this time, making their own debut LP mostly out of date with themselves...

'Road Runner' (Ellas McDaniel aka Bo Diddly)

A professional and polished opener to the album rather than a raw rocker, this is a respectable cover of Bo Diddly's 1960 hit inspired by the Wile E. Coyote And The Road Runner cartoons. In some ways, the song is a novelty track and perhaps doesn't deserve the rather earnest musings about how it lets down The Zombies' oeuvre. Of their RnB covers, Claes Johansen went so far as to say that '[they] ought never to have seen the light of day, not even retrospectively' – and he's a fan! Blunstone commented sensibly to me in 2009: 'With the exception of 'Summertime', I think the covers are a bit weak, but it is worth remembering that they were recorded at breakneck speed by a band that was at the very beginning of its artistic journey'.

The covers are mostly worth more than a casual listen. The howled 'I'm a roadrunner, honey!', complete with a joyous chase down the guitar's neck, means the track is an obvious opener. That fact that respected pianist Otis Spann played on Diddly's cut is also another reason why it would appeal to the band – and Argent in particular – and why they would cover 'Sticks And Stones', which he also featured on. The Zombies do inject more energy than the slower Diddly version, but theirs is perhaps an overzealous take compared with his cool delivery. Yet, The Zombies' deft control of shifting rhythms is immediately evident with some inventive drum fills on display.

The possibilities of this being an attention-grabbing opener weren't lost on other bands; The Pretty Things also opened their debut and eponymous album, released a month prior to *Begin Here*, with a garage version of the track, enhanced by a great Phil May vocal, taking the crown for best cover. Again, The Zombies are behind the times because of this.

Other critics have had some extreme views on the RnB covers in the band's catalogue, with Alec Palao saying that they're some of the *best* UK versions of these tracks and many others feeling they're a blight on The Zombies' career. The truth is really in between the two viewpoints. At a time when pop LPs were only just beginning to move away from simply being a record of the band's live performance, it's difficult to see how The Zombies couldn't have included some of these types of tracks. Moreover, they can just be seen as artefacts in The Zombies' quest for their sound, or indeed, just as a bit of fun! At least the album version packs a punch, which can't be said for the *Saturday Club* performance from autumn 1964, which has the band temporarily intimated by their surroundings, particularly apparent in Atkinson's cautious guitar lines.

'Summertime' (George Gershwin, Ira Gershwin, Du Bose Heyward, Dorothy Heyward)
Whilst Summertime makes for a haunting closing to the Zombies EP, it's a canny bit of track ordering that it's the second song on this album, as it forms a kind of A/B side displaying the thumping RnB band on the one hand and the cool jazzers on the other.

'I Can't Make Up My Mind' (Chris White)
The first two tracks seem designed to exemplify The Zombies as both beat group and balladeers, making for a savvy marketing choice but a fairly safe opening to the album. Their first original composition arrives on track three: it's worth waiting for. It marks their earliest use of 12-string guitar, adding just a hint of muscle to the arrangement and it's an effective follow-on from 'Summertime', continuing the brooding mood. The shrewd echo on Blunstone's vocal creates a clarity to contrast with the slumberous 'Summertime' and the keening backing harmonies intensify the angst.

It's classic Zombies cool: a shade of The Kinks' 'Set Me Free' hovering, an effortless, almost shrugging guitar solo and that familiar use of minor to major shifts. The drier guitar tone with little sustain adds a chilly feel, but the tone is slightly sharper and brighter in the intro than in the solo, which has muddier notes, keeping a sense of indecision as outlined in the title. Whilst the lyrics might seem unremarkable at first glance, there's a progression from previous ones in which we now hear from the girlfriend: 'She said, "Why don't you come back to me?"' etc. and the band are moving away from love songs in which they're mostly betrayed by their mates rather than their lovers, towards a more mature outlook.

When I asked Blunstone about how much he'd worked out the phrasing of his vocal delivery beforehand, he replied via email in 2009: 'For the most part at this time in my career, I just sang off the top of my head. There wasn't any planning that went into phrasing. Very different to how I record now, by the way…' Although, he did mention how the wordiness of some tracks meant they could be a challenge. Whilst the phrasing might not have been consciously decided, controlled and understated, performances like this suggest an instinctive understanding of what the music required.

'The Way I Feel Inside' (Rod Argent)
Argent has spun the tale behind this track many times: he wrote it on the toilet and nearly missed the tour bus, but it doesn't detract from the song's sweetness! Making use of diminished chords to enhance the singer's isolation as he wrangles with expressing his feelings or not, this track stands out on the album.

Ken Jones had the idea of an almost acapella performance, possibly influenced by the intro of 'Sometimes', and he also added the sound effects of footsteps and a coin, making it seem as if the song is being busked, or possibly that the singer's fate will be decided by the flip of a coin. The track would have worked better if it had remained without any backing at all, as it has a rather pedestrian arrangement with an overly church sound on the organ: perhaps a pun on acappella, which in Italian means in the church style. However, it was admired by the band, and it shares a similar atmosphere to the Argent/White composition 'Her Song' from Blunstone's swooning 1971 album *One Year*. White would further experiment with other acapella arrangements with the help of The Kings Singers on the track 'Wonderful' from Blunstone's 1974 solo album *Journey*, which he also produced. 'Wonderful' was released as a single but failed to chart.

Blunstone recollected to me in 2009: "The Way I Feel Inside' was a bit of a challenge as, without any instrumentation, I had to stay in perfect tune throughout the song so that when the backing comes in at the end, we're all playing in the same key'.

The demo of this track on *Zombie Heaven,* with its full backing, makes the debt to The Beatles' 'If I Fell' too evident and they were wise to plump for a sparser and so more innovative arrangement. However, the demo also reveals the band bantering about the title, with one suggestion being 'The Way I Feel Myself Tonight'…

'Work 'n' Play' (Ken Jones)

This was written by their Mancunian producer Ken Jones, a conductor and composer who would later write the themes for sitcoms *Sykes* and *Only When I Laugh*. Jones suggested that the album needed an instrumental for variety, although the more astute members of the band felt this was more a ploy for a cut of the royalties! Argent plays a spirited harmonica, despite being new to the instrument – albeit he'd experimented with one as a child. The fade-in at the start is said to have been inspired by The Beatles' 'Eight Days A Week'.

'You Really Got A Hold On Me/Bring It On Home To Me' (Smokey Robinsons/Sam Cooke)

These two tracks formed a medley on the snappily titled *The Miracles Recorded Live On The Stage*. Written by Smokey Robinson, 'You Really Got A Hold On Me' was a favourite with many beat bands, including The Beatles, who performed it on their second album, *With The Beatles,* in 1964. Its use of 7th chords may explain The Zombies' admiration for the track. They wanted to be the first to take Robinson's 'My Girl' into the charts, but The Temptations got there before them at the end of 1964 and so The Zombies decided against recording their own version. A demo was made but has since been lost somewhere in the archives. Blunstone, however, would revisit the Robinson songbook when he released a faithful cover of 'Tracks Of My Tears' in 1982.

The seductively yearning 'You've Really Got A Hold On Me' seems like an obvious choice of cover, but the band follow the original a little too closely to realise it properly. The Beatles' recent cover, which is also reasonably close to the original, ranks amongst their best because of Lennon's excellent and sincere vocal. Whilst Blunstone is fine, The Zombies' attempt is dragged down further by the addition of Sam Cooke's 'Bring It On Home', which is a song that can border on the dirge if not done sharply. Overall, The Zombies' version of both songs seems like a lost opportunity; if we imagine an arrangement with more keyboard and jazz inflections, it could have been something special.

'She's Not There' (Rod Argent)

Although explored in detail previously, it is worth looking at this masterpiece in terms of the role it played on The Zombies' debut LP. Closing the first side was a dramatic flourish, but it also further illuminates the naivety of some of the cover versions. Whilst I feel the criticism of those has been hyperbolic, it's difficult to take those songs as seriously when ranked alongside this track. Yet, the fact that almost a year had passed between the single's issue and the album's release highlights how timing was a problem for the band, and how having no reserve of original material to draw on proved a significant hindrance.

'Sticks And Stones' (Titus Turner)

Opening the second half with a rocky number follows the early format of album track sequencing in the 1960s, with albums being put together more like live shows. This bouncy opener was written by Titus Turner, who also penned 'Leave My Kitten Alone', one of the best previously unreleased tracks on *The Beatles Anthology*, incidentally.

The band knew this cut from the Ray Charles version, which is a more mature take on it. The Zombies, however, turn it into an insolent howl with a great swirling organ solo that conjures the atmosphere of a circus (something Argent would revisit with his eponymous band from the 1970s) shadowed by some vibrant garage guitar licks. Essentially, the lyrics recount how scandal and rumour are attempting to break up his relationship, but words won't ever be that powerful; on the downside, Blunstone's vocal is a rare misfire, being mannered and strained. However, the track boots open the second half, breaking the pensive tension left by 'She's Not There'.

'Sticks And Stones' has been covered by a crowd of other artists, including Jerry Lee Lewis, The Kingsmen, who deliver a sparky take on the track, and brassy, bellowing versions from Joe Cocker and Elvis Costello. However, The Zombies don't add the backing vocals on the 'I've been abused' refrain as all others do and instead have Blunstone holding the note, creating a piercingly raw feel that redeems the rest of his vocal performance.

'Can't Nobody Love You' (Phillip Mitchell)

Solomon Burke's version was most familiar to the band, but it was written by James Mitchell, probably best known as the songwriter of 'Hurt So

Good', which was recorded by Susan Cadogan in 1975. Short of material, Blunstone recalled hearing this for the first time only the day before they decided to record it.

The Zombies' version has a country feel with a strong and controlled vocal by Blunstone, who's back in gear here, but despite the polished performance and production, it isn't that memorable and smacks of filler, especially on the US release, where it takes up space that an Argent or White composition could have filled better. Nevertheless, the later incarnation of The Zombies would make this a regular of their live shows and Blunstone's vocals are always sincere but controlled.

'Woman' (Rod Argent)

This throwback to the Zombies EP picks up the energy but really is another indication that the band weren't ready to record an LP. In all fairness, long players and not *albums* were the order of the day, but just one or two tweaks in the track listing could have made this an outstanding debut. When teamed with the previous two tracks, it's clear that the second half is weaker and the most dated in its sound.

'I Don't Want To Know' (Chris White)

Another White track with Atkinson on 12-string guitar, and a rustling, picked intro that has a hint of The Byrds, this changes the mood and brings The Zombies out of an early 1960s sound into a more forward-looking one. The song tells of how the protagonist refuses to hear the bad things that his friends say about his girl, inverting the lyrics of 'She's Not There', which mourn a lack of advice. The track also follows 'Tell Her No' on *The Zombies* and it's almost a response, with the speaker wanting to deny that song's guidance.

This is also another track showing how sparingly the organ could be used to vary what could become a predictable sound, and if we think of other bands with keyboardists, such as The Animals, the organ can sometimes dominate too much. Instead, The Zombies maintain a delicacy here. The verse accompaniment drops in intensity for the chorus, creating an interesting twist and hinting at the futility of the lyrics, whilst the muscular bridge is, in some ways, more of a chorus – this trademark would reoccur on other recordings.

'I Remember When I Loved Her' (Rod Argent)

Looking forward to the summer-to-early-winter soundscape of *Odessey And Oracle*, this exquisite ballad shouldn't be tucked away here. The lyrics are more sophisticated than their wider company, as in 'Now we are strange/No more in love', meaning strange in the sense of estranged, but also drawing attention to how being out of love is an uncanny experience à la 'She's Not There', enhanced by another controlled use of diminished chords. The frosty percussion increases the cooling of love that is echoed in the verse: 'She seems so cold to me/But I remember when I loved her'. An ethereal and brief keyboard solo expresses how their love has been spirited away so easily. In June 1965, the track was the B-side for the US-only release of 'I Want You Back Again'.

The dedicated Ola And The Janglers covered this, matching Blunstone's lamenting cadences almost exactly. Meanwhile, Germany's The Boots renamed it 'When I Loved Her', adding twangy guitars.

'What More Can I Do' (Chris White)

This being the UK B-side to 'Tell Her No', it might seem odd to choose this over the A-side, but in terms of shaking up the sound of the lesser half of the album, this gets the job done. It's a blunt shift after the fragility of the previous track and displays how the band were in a position to write songs just as frenetic as the ones they were choosing to cover.

'I Got My Mojo Working' (Preston Foster, McKinley Morganfield, aka Muddy Waters)

Although this track was made famous by Muddy Waters' adaptation, Ann Cole first recorded it in 1956. The song tells of how the protagonist has a magic charm to win love, but the object of desire is still managing to resist. In hoodoo, the charm or the mojo could be made from fingernails, hair and twigs, but needs a spirit to release its power. A band with a link to voodoo in their name would surely be drawn to a song with such strong blues iconography, but this track is often held up as evidence of how weak The Zombies' covers are. There's also an argument for how some white performers simply can't convince when dipping into another culture; there could be something absurd about a few lads from St. Albans attempting these types of songs. Whether the many bands who covered blues songs at this time could truly engage lyrically, it was obvious that the music spoke to them, and all of The Zombies were vivified by their first hearings of both blues and rock 'n' roll from artists such as John Lee Hooker to Ray Charles, from Little Richard to Elvis Presley. In reality, there's an elation in their performance that is only ever found on a band's early recordings, when the sheer joy of making a noise is abundant. Argent takes an unabashed lead vocal that might be unsophisticated but is enthusiastic and energetic. He asked Jones if he could re-record it, as he was dismayed when he heard the playback but wasn't given the chance. Yet, Argent's squalling harmonica emphasises the energy and Atkinson puts forth his most Harrison-esque solo. In some ways, this is The Zombies doing a cover of The Beatles doing a cover!

Bringing the album to a close, it might not go out with the bang the band were aiming for, but it keeps the feeling of a 'live artefact' going well and the US album closes with the same track too.

Conclusion

Begin Here isn't going to make the Top Ten best debut albums (although a solid argument could be made for the best debut single in 'She's Not There'), yet its parent album bears repeated listening and perhaps more *attentive* listening than might at first seem to be required. It can certainly be said that some of the sounds are prescient, with hints of The Byrds, The Doors and Procol Harum winking here and there. And for its £200 recording fee, it's certainly worth it.

For the US release, entitled simply *The Zombies*, it's evident that side one is the strongest, but the second half cannily opens with 'Tell Her No', which would have bolstered the UK version. Overall, though, the track ordering is a little regretful, as casual listeners probably played the first couple of numbers on each side, leaving some great tracks unexplored. Yet, it still roughly follows the outline of what a live set would do. And at least it's not stuffed with instrumentals as Capital did to The Beatles' early US releases. It certainly fared better than the UK version too, as it made the Top 40 in the album charts.

The Singles 1965

Now it gets complicated, as it'll be nearly three years before The Zombies release another album. Whilst this was obviously to their detriment, it did allow them to become powerful live performers who were always a big draw regardless of where they were in the charts.

Not only did they find success in America, but the band were growing a loyal following in Scandinavia and embarked on a short tour in the winter of 1964. It was the first time that Grundy had flown and he was dreading the flight. Yet, it certainly seems worth the journey as they secured a dedicated audience there. Also, rumour has it that The Zombies were 'impressed' by Scandinavian groupies, with one – Trondheim Lil – leaving her mark especially. Chris White told Johnny Black: 'Coming back in the snow from Trondheim, which is North of the Arctic Circle, we saw this girl walking along. So we picked her up and we nicknamed her Trondheim Lil. Before long, the road manager had made a list of the hotel rooms for her to visit. And she did'.

There were also numerous tours in the US. Playing up to eight shows a day, and often trapped in the venue because of rabid fans, The Zombies found it a very different experience from what they were used to in the UK. It was also a fruitful time for learning from others as they shared bills with Patti Labelle And The Bluebells, The Drifters and The Shangri Las. Grundy would occasionally ride the motorbike onto the stage before 'Leader Of The Pack', whilst Argent was tasked with being kissed by vocalist Mary Weiss for 'Give Him A Great Big Kiss'.

Not only were the shows lively, but backstage was entertaining too. Blunstone told Johnny Black:

They (Patti Labelle And The Bluebells) invited me for a drink in their room and while I was there, Cindy suddenly had an epileptic fit, shaking and rolling on the floor. She had her hairbrush clenched in her teeth and it was quite terrifying. Then they just cracked up laughing. They took us in one by one and she would do it every time.

After having such a big hit with 'She's Not There', it seemed that the band should focus on maintaining their US fan base, but what had made The Zombies exotic and noticeable was in danger of being diluted by so much live work. The British Invasion had taken the US in its grip, a great opportunity for the band to exploit this as much as they could. The British Invasion was the nickname given to the seemingly endless barrage of UK bands who were taking over the *Cashbox* and *Billboard* charts. Although The Beatles are, of course, the most notable of these bands, the first stirrings of the invasion had already begun as early as 1952 with Vera Lynn's 'Aufweidesehn, Sweetheart' topping the charts, and then instrumentals by Acker Bilk and The Tornados following suit at the start of the sixties. However, these were seen as one-offs as the tracks didn't have much in common, with Bilk's easy listening against the proto space pop of 'Telstar'. Overall, the music was reasonably safe, as it didn't directly reference rock 'n' roll or R&B or anything that could be said to be exactly America's own. But The Beatles, The Dave Clark Five, The Rolling Stones, The Animals, etc., were not only covering tracks by the rock 'n' roll masters, such as Elvis Presley, Chuck Berry and Little Richard, but they were acknowledging influences before them by referring to blues players and country and western acts, and also performing tracks by contemporary US girl groups. In short, they were reflecting the past of US pop *and* its present with little effort. They also appeared to be suggesting its future by showing how bands could sing and play at the same time, and, in some cases, by proving that they could compose songs too. In terms of The Zombies, they also had something different: their jazz leanings were one area where the invasion bands hadn't quite managed to take hold. By pushing The Zombies into countless live sets that required them to take on all of the genres being mastered by the invaders so that they would still sound current, it's easy to see how a sense of identity could be hard to maintain. For many bands, versatility would lead to longevity, but for The Zombies, we can clearly see how their diverse singles might make it hard for the casual listener to recognise them.

Yet, their live dates certainly strengthened their already tight musicianship and allowed them to perform alongside others who would inspire the continued development of both their recordings and songwriting. The Dick Clark Tour began with Clark quoted by Peter Jones in *Record Mirror*: 'They are the BEST group, artistically, I have ever seen'. Dick Clark's *Caravan Of Stars* started in 1959 as a live spin-off from Clark's music show *American Bandstand,* which boasted acts such as Paul Anka and Bobby Vee, along with The Coasters and The Drifters.

Hugh Grundy elaborated to *Goldmine*:

It was a sort of two-headed tour: we were headlining one part of it and Herman's Hermits were headlining the other part. We toured all over the States. We played every other night for about five or six weeks. The two tours coincided in Toronto and we all played a big theatre. I do remember distinctly being down in the dressing room that night and it was exactly like *Spinal Tap*: we couldn't find our way up to the stage. We were going down corridors saying, is this where we're supposed to go? Meanwhile, we could hear the roar of the crowd from upstairs as we tried to find the stage!

However, The Zombies were pioneers, being the first UK act signed for the tour despite a delay caused by their wait for visas. UK acts that followed included Herman's Hermits, Peter And Gordon and Tom Jones. The band joined the caravan in Nashville, beginning in the spring of 1965. Joining them for the first leg were Del Shannon, The Ikettes, DeeDee Sharp, The

Shangri-Las, Tommy Roe, The Ad Libs, The Velvettes and Mel Carter, who all performed at Municipal Auditorium together, as well as the lesser-recalled The Larks, Jimmy Soul, The Executives, Jewel Aikens and Mike Clifford.

Not only were The Zombies learning about music and showmanship, but also about the politics of a place they'd longed to visit. Paul Atkinson told *Goldmine*:

We came back to the States in July of '65 with the Searchers. I remember one show in Virginia we did with Peter And Gordon, Tom Jones, The Beach Boys and The Searchers. It was wild. That was our introduction to the Deep South and playing to segregated audiences. I remember playing Montgomery, Alabama and getting a shock because, backstage before the show, the bathrooms were marked 'white male', 'black male', 'white female', 'black female'. When we went onstage and looked out at the audience, they were segregated. The audience came in through separate entrances, sat in separate seating areas and went to separate bathrooms. It was only then that it really came home to me: some of the people on the tour were people we idolised, like The Isleys. And we would go into a fast food restaurant and we'd sit down, and they wouldn't serve us. And finally, we would say, can we get a menu or something? And they would say quite openly, 'If you would like to ask your friends to leave, then we'll be happy to serve you'. It was hard to find a roadside restaurant that would serve all of us. So, frequently, we'd stop twice for lunch — once for them, once for us.

Blunstone formed a friendship with The Velvettes' vocalist Caroline Gill and was warned how this might cause, at best, consternation, if not outright violence, when they went out in public together, which they continued to do.

However, the conflicts were not just political, as not all of the acts got on well together. Dee Dee Sharp pulled a gun on Mel Carter and was booted off the tour. Chris White alleged to Johnny Black that Sharp had objected to Carter because he was gay.

But, despite multiple live commitments, the band released many well-crafted singles.

I Want You Back Again b/w I Remember When I Loved Her

Personnel:
Colin Blunstone: lead vocals
Rod Argent: keyboards, backing vocals
Chris White: bass, backing vocals
Paul Atkinson: guitar
Hugh Grundy: drums
Recorded: Decca Studios London, 2 March 1965
Producer: Ken Jones
US Release Date: 12 June 1965
Chart placings: UK: did not chart, US: 92 (Cashbox) 95 (Billboard)

'I Want You Back Again' (Rod Argent)

Decca were unhappy with this as a choice of single, feeling that it lacked commercial appeal, and it marked the start of the company doubting the band's ability to write their own hits. The track was only released as a single in the US and it has to be said that the 6/4 timing isn't the most appealing of sounds in terms of earworms, in my opinion, and it's a more complex listen than the average pop song, yet similar comments could have been made of 'She's Not There'. Perhaps a song like this doesn't work if only a brief snippet is heard on the radio, as it is both sophisticated and naïve, with John Mendelsohn describing it as 'a supper club jazzer'. Writing the foreword to *The Zombies Odessey* book, Tom Petty said the band's sound 'was so original it hurt'. It could be argued that it also hurt the band because it impacted their commercial appeal. Nevertheless, Petty also had a special admiration for this track and performed a stunning live version that surely influenced The Zombies' remake (it reappears on *Still Got That Hunger* in 2015) with its extended and aggressive keyboard solo. It's available on *Tom Petty: The Live Anthology* from 2009. The Zombies themselves didn't play the track live, possibly deterred by its challenging rhythm.

The complexities of this track also link to another problem – how did record stores categorise the band? Blunstone elaborated to me: 'In America, the retailer would order from wholesale and they had people called rackers – they would rack by the type of music. This sounds so bizarre, but if they didn't know where to rack your album, that was a problem. Little things like that can hold you back'.

However, there are successful details in their first version: the looser drum fills that counter the clockwork rhythm are clever and the inclusion of flat chords adds an unexpected flavour to the chorus. The alternative version on *Zombie Heaven* is very similar to the released one but with a less confident keyboard solo. However, the most compelling version is definitely the powerful reworking on *Still Got That Hunger*.

'I Remember When I Loved Her' (Rod Argent)

This delicate Argent composition was also a track on *Begin Here*. It might have made for a more successful (if less original) A-side, sharing a pleasing melancholy with earlier Zombies songs.

Whenever You're Ready b/w **I Love You**

Personnel
Colin Blunstone: lead vocals,
Rod Argent: keyboards, backing vocals,
Chris White: bass, backing vocals
Paul Atkinson: guitar
Hugh Grundy: drums
Recorded: Decca Studios London, 24 June 1965

Producer: Ken Jones
UK Release Date: 3 September 1965
US Release Date: 26 November 1965
Chart placings: UK: did not chart; US: 114 (Cashbox) 110 (Billboard)

'Whenever You're Ready' (Rod Argent)

Argent was inspired by The Impressions, whose 'It's Alright' might have also provided a previous influence, at least lyrically. The Zombies were big fans, also covering 'You Must Believe Me' and 'People Get Ready', with the latter informing this track. It's a mature song, augmented by an elegant melody, and it came as a shock to the band when it didn't enter the UK chart and merely brushed the US Top 100. This was also in spite of continued confidence in The Zombies from the music press: *Cashbox* commented, 'The Zombies should have no difficulty in zooming up the Hitsville path lickety-split with this ultra-commercial Parrot offering...' The record-buying public's reception to the track increased their frustration with Jones, as the band were unable to take part in the mixing of this track and felt the recorded version lacked what they'd captured in their live performances. The demo proves slightly different, being a fraction faster, and the keyboard is less prominent in the mix, but these minor variations demonstrate how thoughtfully and thoroughly the songs were worked out beforehand. Nevertheless, there is still a fruitful spontaneity to Argent's solos in both versions.

This is another 'well' song ('Well, I've been hurt but I still love you'), with the singer waiting for a sincere token of love – and there's just a shiver of pessimism in the gorgeous fall of the melody in the chorus. Perhaps the middle eight isn't quite distinct enough from the rest of the song to add anything, but the restive hiss of the cymbal is a wry comment on the singer's (im)patience. The band must have been just as impatient, as it really should have been a hit. Blunstone later said that the quality of the song was better than the recording, but it's a sterling effort.

'I Love You' (Chris White)

Recorded: 8 July 1965

Another minor to major song, this was sparked by the music that the band were hearing as part of the Dick Clark Tour. Opening with the chorus, it's an arresting track, heightened by the unease of the off-beat and the thoughtful use of an uncertain-sounding 6th chord, reflecting the singer's inarticulate state. Whilst the title might be unequivocal, once again, the speaker is frustrated by not being able to express themselves. It's likely to have made for a preferable A-side, particularly if the number of cover versions it led to are considered. There's also an alternative mono version by The Zombies that includes an intro not found on other reissues, and whilst interesting to hear, the burst of chorus is the most powerful opening. Derek Johnson in the *NME* described the song as 'most competent', and whilst this is faint praise in this instance, it does apply to a number of Zombies recordings that are well performed and constructed but lacking... *something*. Here, however, I don't think that's quite right, although it might be argued that the drums are too light.

The song is unexpectedly important in the band's catalogue because of the impact of a particular cover version: the Californian band People! covered it in 1968, and it became a number-one hit in Japan. Adding a tense extended intro, their version pushes the four-minute mark and displays a 'Time Of The Season' style organ solo and some tautly dramatic pauses. In fact, People! Zombify it all the more. However, it was actually a Japanese band, The Carnabeats, who'd covered it first in 1967, calling it 'Sukisa', speeding it up and making it sound more like The Animals. Mexico's Los Chijuas performed the song as the penultimate track on their eponymous album, but stuck closer to the People! version. The Zombies cut was re-released in 1968, backed with 'The Way I Feel Inside' as a result of People!'s moderate success. Some sources claim that this meant the recording company didn't completely give up on releasing tracks from *Odessey And Oracle,* which meant 'Time of the Season' could be a hit.

Therefore, it's no wonder that The Zombies have a fondness for the track, often opening their shows with it to this day. That arrangement owes something to People!'s version, with suspenseful pauses and the slight increase in speed demonstrating a pleasing resemblance to The Beatles' 'Things We Said Today'. Several powerful live versions are available, all showing that Blunstone's vocals still have an astonishing purity.

Is This The Dream b/w Don't Go Away

Personnel:
Colin Blunstone: lead vocals
Rod Argent: keyboards, backing vocals
Chris White: bass, backing vocals
Paul Atkinson: guitar
Hugh Grundy: drums
Producer: Ken Jones
Recorded: Landsdowne Studios
UK Release Date: 26 November 1965
US Release Date: 28 February 1966
Chart placings: UK: did not chart, US: did not chart

'Is This The Dream' (Rod Argent)
Recorded: 10 November 1965
This track, which again revisits the theme of absence and yearning, was favourably reviewed by George Harrison for *Blind Date* in December 1965 – 'I've got a soft spot for The Zombies. I've liked most of their records, I specifically like the electric piano on this'. However, he doubted that it would

climb the charts and he was sadly prophetic. Interestingly, the track shares another connection with Harrison, as the lyric "Cause baby, you'll just cry for a shadow' echoes the title of a Beatles instrumental written by Harrison and Lennon in the style of The Shadows. This image of futility, in some ways, is also a lyrical influence on 'She's Not There', and a number of early tracks before culminating in the desperately tragic longing on 'A Rose For Emily'.

Whilst it is lyrically very much in the style of The Zombies, they felt that the recording didn't represent their sound, with Argent telling Tom Doyle in 2016:

Ken Jones would never let us stay for the mix. I remember leaving the session and us all thinking, 'That sounds fantastic'. We went down to the pub and then came back about three hours later when he had mixed it, and I remember thinking, 'Has somebody else come in and recorded this?' It was just not as we remembered it. So we got very frustrated with that.

Argent later revealed to Dorian Lynskey from *The Guardian* in 2008 that Jones 'had mixed the balls out of the subsequent singles'. Blunstone told me in 2009: 'We owe an awful lot to Ken Jones. The only problem was that he was always trying to re-make 'She's Not There', and didn't realise that the band were growing and changing'.

Yet, immediately, this is an ear-catching song, and it's much harder to understand why the public ignored it. In a fairer world, it would be regarded almost as a northern soul classic, with its hints of The Marvellettes and The Spencer Davies-style stomping in the verses. The band play exceptionally well, with a propellant bass and tumbling, but controlled drumming. Despite the group's disappointment with the mix, the track is powerfully built and displays a new thicker and slightly distorted guitar sound, with the keyboard solo squawking more like a harmonica.

'Don't Go Away' (Chris White)
Recorded: 24 June 1965

This is a gorgeous B-side with a shade of The Rolling Stones' 'Tell Me' that was originally entitled 'You'll Go Away'. Characterised by rich and sweet harmonies, it also blends jangling guitar with a plangent bassline that complements the lyrics' use of light and dark imagery. The line 'Daylight and the new light' is an apposite description of Blunstone's tone here, as his vocals are at once gleaming but soft. It's clear that The Zombies' B-sides were often of a higher standard than many A-sides by their contemporaries (the week that this was released saw generic tracks from Len Barry, Chris Andrews and The Fortunes dominate the Top Ten). Therefore, it is understandable that the band became jaded by both a lack of commercial success and because of restricted control over their work.

The Singles 1966

This will prove a brave kingdom to me, where I shall have my music for nothing.
Stefano, William Shakespeare, *The Tempest*

Despite limited success in the UK, The Zombies' profile was large enough in the US that they were offered the chance to compose and record three songs for the thriller *Bunny Lake Is Missing,* directed by the renowned Otto Preminger. On the surface, this seemed like an unmissable opportunity and surely one that would send their star into the ascendant, but bad luck dragged them back to earth again.

Whilst the songs were recorded in early 1965, the film's US release came in the autumn of the year, with the UK release waiting until February 1966. This meant that The Zombies' sound had shifted yet again and these singles were not indicative of it. Moreover, the director proved to be insufferable, as Colin Blunstone recalled to Brian Greene for *It's Psychedelic, Baby* magazine in 2015:

Otto Preminger was a very demanding and aggressive man. He was very tough on the film crew and his staff, but it didn't really work with us, as we didn't really mind if we were included in the film or not. When he realised that he couldn't bully us, he quietened down and was much more reasonable. I wish we had had more time to work on the songs. We were asked to write and record three new songs in about ten days. If we'd had more time, I think we could have come up with stronger material.

Argent told *Goldmine* regarding Preminger: 'He was a sod, actually. He was a real swine, a very unpleasant man, I thought. We got the part in the film by auditioning for him. We actually played 'Summertime' and I think he used to love Gershwin, as I subsequently heard. He was impressed by the fact that we had played 'Summertime''. To make things worse, although the band appeared on screen for less than a minute, it took them *two days* to film the segment. However, what an opportunity for Blunstone, whose first-ever composition was played in the back of a scene with Laurence Olivier! Although, the band, alas, didn't actually get to meet any of the actors.

Bluntone's success might also have started to widen a crack within the band, as there were now three songwriters who would be able to secure a bigger cut of royalties and two members who wouldn't. It has to be remembered that Blunstone only wrote twice for The Zombies, but it did imply an extra talent he could fall back on, other than performing. For Grundy and Atkinson, this wasn't the case, with Atkinson admitting to Johansen: 'I tried really hard, and I did write some things, but they were very, very clichéd and obviously very derivative of distinct songs'.

Therefore, The Zombies began the year in the UK with a retrospective step that would set the trend once again for the rest of the year. When their second UK single of 1966 emerged, 'Indication', it was evident that the band had moved on. Even with innovative and forward-looking tracks, sales were inexplicably low, and for the first time, the band released cover versions as singles. This might have seemed a better bet, but caused confusion yet again: who were The Zombies? What did they stand for? There are strong Zombies releases to be found in the year 1966, but comparing them to their contemporaries is revealing on this occasion. In the year of *Blonde On Blonde*, *Pet Sounds*, *Freak Out* and *Revolver*, the year when, quite possibly, the album truly became an artistic statement, a lack of any album at all is deeply unfortunate.

Yet, it has to be noted that many British Invasion bands saw their fortunes dip at this time. A few, like Herman's Hermits, managed hits into mid-1967, but many saw their singles stall in the latter half of the Top 100. The Beatles' final shows at Candlestick Park in August 1966 are a bit too convenient to describe as the ending of the glut of Brit acts, but it does indicate a watershed. There's also the shift from British pop acts to rock acts having hits across the Atlantic. Louis Criscione wrote for *KRLA Beat* on 28 May 1966:

> People such as The Honeycombs, Searchers, Zombies, Gerry And The Pacemakers, Billy J. Kramer, Sounds Incorporated, The Moody Blues, The Seekers, Freddie And The Dreamers and The Unit Four Plus Two came and went so fast that their departure was hardly even noticed. Now it's Spring of '66, roughly 27 months since the British invasion began, and the Americans are again ruling the roost. Now, the English singers on the charts are the exceptions instead of the other way around.

Blunstone had also noticed a change in the way the band were received, telling *Record Mirror*'s Peter Jones in 1966:

> In the old days (last month!), my main concern was keeping out of reach of the clutching hands of girls at the edge of the stage. And getting off the stage without being torn to pieces. Now, it's like a cold war. They just stand there, hardly breathing, staring straight at us, rocking backwards and forwards and tapping to the beat. It's more gratifying musically, but I must say I enjoyed the gigs where the audience screamed the roofs down.

However, The Zombies star was still rising elsewhere across the globe and they were given the chance to tour the Philippines. It was not auspicious, though, as The Beatles had decided to quit touring partly in response to their treatment in this country. Argent told Tom Cox for *Uncut* in 1997: 'I remember when our manager suggested that we tour the Philippines. He guaranteed we wouldn't lose any money, so we went along with it. We were playing to 45,000-seat arenas and making 80 quid a night. I know the promoter of that tour made at least £26,000 net profit'.

Blunstone elaborated to Jordan Runtagh at *People*, 2017:

We didn't know we'd had any hit records in the Far East, so when we arrived at like two o'clock in the morning, there was a huge crowd as we got off the plane and there was a lot of excitement. I can remember looking over my shoulder and thinking, 'There must be someone famous on this plane'. It was us! It was two o'clock in the morning and thousands of people were there. I thought we were going to play in a hotel bar in the evenings and we'd get a chance to sunbathe and have a swim during the day – that's what I was expecting.

When The Zombies returned to the UK, they were ready for new management, a new record deal and the chance to produce themselves.

Remember You b/w Just Out of Reach (UK Version), Just Out of Reach b/w Remember You (US Version)

Personnel:
Colin Blunstone: lead vocals,
Rod Argent: keyboards, backing vocals,
Chris White: bass, backing vocals
Paul Atkinson: guitar
Hugh Grundy: drums
Recorded: Decca Studios London, 2 March 1965
Producer: Ken Jones
UK Release Date: 21 January 1966
US Release Date: 25 October 1965
Chart placings: UK: did not chart, US: 114 (Cashbox) 110 (Billboard)

'Just Out Of Reach' (Colin Blunstone)

It was an extraordinary opportunity for the band: recording songs for the hotly anticipated mystery *Bunny Lake Is Missing*, starring Carol Lynley and Keir Dullea, but Argent's well had temporarily run dry. Therefore, White wrote two of the tracks, leaving Blunstone to write this one: the only one actually featured in the film and not just on the soundtrack album. Sadly, for Blunstone, the recording wasn't as exciting as it might have been, with Preminger interfering and Gus Dudgeon recalling that the director behaved like 'an absolute arsehole'. Bizarrely, Preminger was offended first by the recording equipment and then later picked a fight with the band when they were miming to the trailer jingle after he'd asked them to… mime to the trailer jingle. No matter, this is a catchy pop song, if uncomplicated, which has a strong hook in the chorus – it opens the song as 'I Love You' does.

It's an unassuming lyric, in which his girl is playing hard to get, but it does include an unusual word for a pop song: 'inattentively'.

Sylvia Stephens, writing for *Fabulous* in 1965, described the band miming on a mock-up of the *Ready Steady Go!* set whilst Preminger looked down from atop a ladder. She also recollected that Blunstone told her he'd been up since half past five rehearsing the song by himself, as he was anxious about the performance. He later said that the band were not that intimidated...

It must also have been satisfying for Blunstone that his debut as a songwriter was covered by Jamaica's Jackie Edwards (who wrote 'Keep On Running' as released by The Spencer Davis Group), who recorded it in 1967.

Preminger was concerned about the twist in the film being revealed if patrons saw the ending before the rest of the film, so decided to use this as part of the marketing as Hitchcock had done for *Psycho*. Therefore, The Zombies re-recorded 'Just Out Of Reach' as 'Come On Time', available on *Zombie Heaven*. The reworked lyrics are camp, to say the least: 'Otto Preminger presents Bunny Lake Is Missing/What suspense! Laurence Olivier is immense!' The arch performance might be a swipe at the bullying director, who also berated Blunstone for his English pronunciation of clock. In frustration, Argent overexaggerated the word, yawling 'clarrrk!' If you've ever wondered what a mash-up of The Zombies and The Bonzo Dog Band (a unique British group who blended music hall and jazz in the 1960s) would sound like, you're quids in here.

'Remember You' (Chris White)

This was not included in the film, but it, nevertheless, found a place on the soundtrack album that also contained a score by Paul Glass, whose father was the silent film actor Gaston Glass.

This is another song in waltz time, but it was inspired by music from Churchill's funeral! In fact, it has a shade of 'If You Want To Make A Fool Of Somebody' by James Ray and covered by Freddie And The Dreamers. It's an interesting listen, but a bewildering choice for an A-side, being at least two years behind in its sound. Of note is the change in Argent's keyboard tone, as it has a thinner, more rock 'n' roll sound.

The lyrics recount memories of a past love, but whilst being little on the page, they do adhere to the music well enough and White certainly isn't guilty of cramming too many words in, as Blunstone would sometimes point out to him regarding other songs.

The version on *Zombie Heaven* has the band bantering and breaking into a brief chorus of Frank Ifield's 'I Remember You'. There's an appealing use of harps that lift what could be a predictable, almost nursery rhyme melody, and the band keep a firm grip on the slipping/sliding feel from verse to chorus with deft control. The heavier arrangement on the box set gives a power that makes it the preferable performance, however.

Indication b/w How We Were Before

Personnel:
Colin Blunstone: lead vocals
Rod Argent: keyboards, backing vocals
Chris White: bass, backing vocals
Paul Atkinson: guitar
Hugh Grundy: drums
Producer: Ken Jones
UK Release Date: 17 June 1966
US Release Date: 15 June 1966
Chart placings: UK: did not chart, US: did not chart

'Indication' (Rod Argent)

Recorded: May 1966

Opening with the wry, 'It's not that you're wrong, it's just that I'm right', this song recounts how the singer is trying to hold off his feelings of love. Whilst, lyrically, it may seem to be covering barren ground, musically, it's a mosaic of what had so far defined 1960s pop and indicates (pun intended) where it was headed. The song developed from an onstage jam but is a tightly and meticulously constructed piece.

Opening with a baroque intro, (which may have influenced The Move's debut single 'Night Of Fear' later in the year), its close harmonies recall The Hollies, with the bouncing bass on the verses evoking Motown, and the triumphant chorus building on producer Phil Spector's Wall Of Sound, which used reverb and multiple layering of instruments and voices to create Wagnerian impact.

The song is in two halves, with the pop section first, before an extended psyche fade-out that was severed for radio play, hacking it to just two minutes. But the solo is the highlight of the song, with suspended chords building a tension that's never resolved, cleverly combined with the determined atmosphere of a raga. It might have also worked in a 'Voodoo Chile (Slight Return)' way, with the catchy part and the loose chunk separated. The heavier drumming and the mild distortion of the guitar look ahead to the emerging rock sound, showing that The Zombies were not going to be left behind in terms of their development, if not their record sales. The track caused some disagreement in the band, with Atkinson arguing that it wasn't a sensible choice for a single: despite its brilliance, it wasn't.

However, Grundy believed it could make it. Once again, it seems the track may have suffered because of its disparate parts. It's easy to understand that the casual listener might not always recognise the varied facets of a number of Zombies singles as being of the same whole. Yet when other 1960s classics may have become over-familiar, The Zombies have a trove of songs ready for re-discovery.

'How We Were Before' (Colin Blunstone)
Recorded: 8 July 1966
This Blunstone composition, one of only two he'd write for the band in the 1960s, is a McCartney-esque ballad that reveals a floaty melody and a sweetly pure vocal. In fact, only Blunstone sings on the track. The arrangement owes something to both The Beatles' take on "Til There Was You' and their own 'And I Love Her'. Atkinson's pretty solo is gentle and stays close to the melody. It's a beautifully romantic track guaranteed to raise a smile. If only, it had charted ...

Gotta Get A Hold Of Myself b/w The Way I Feel Inside
Personnel:
Colin Blunstone: lead vocals
Rod Argent: keyboards, backing vocals
Chris White: bass, backing vocals
Paul Atkinson: guitar
Hugh Grundy: drums
Producer: Ken Jones
Chart placings: UK: did not chart, US: did not chart

'Gotta Get A Hold Of Myself' (Clint Ballard Jr; Angela Riela)
Written by Clint Ballard Sr (no relation to sort-of-Zombie and Argent member Russ), he also wrote 'You're No Good', and like that track, this was first recorded by Dee Dee Warwick, sister of Dionne. The co-writer is Angela Riela, who wrote 'Hey Lulu'. This song recounts how the singer is spooked by the spectral presence of their erstwhile lover: 'Late at night I hear footsteps sound down the hall/And I kid myself that you're coming back after all/Telephone rings, but there's no one on the line, no no no'. This evokes the melodrama of 'She's Not There', and The Zombies, becoming disheartened with a lack of success with original material, felt a cover with a link to their own sound might bring more luck. Ken Jones astutely recommended this track to them.

Eric Harvey, writing for *Pitchfork,* described 'She's Not There' and 'Tell Her No' as 'noirish jazz fusion psychodramas', and whilst this seems overstated (at least for 'Tell Her No', perhaps), it's an insightful comment on The Zombies' motif of absence being the cause of present misery. It might also explain why Preminger felt they were right for the twisty *Bunny Lake Is Missing* when there were more obvious (or perhaps more expensive!) options.

The twitchy, paranoid bass drives the track (a wry touch being the running riff as the line about the footsteps is sung) and, wisely, Grundy strips back his drumming so that the bass remains the focus. This might seem like tepid praise, but The Zombies were a band of impeccable taste, rarely over-egging their arrangements and never playing competitively or tediously. Lenny Kay remarked in the closing notes of 1997's *Zombie Heaven*, 'I couldn't tell which Zombie was which, the mark of a truly equal group'. Argent holds back until the close when a few funereal organ notes seal the doom. Blunstone and Argent's voices really begin to blend beautifully here after a short period of incongruence between Blunstone's smoothness and Argent's immature tone, but the swooping 'Telephone rings but there's no one on the line' is both uncanny and gorgeous. All this results in The Zombies' most successful cover.

It's decidedly unfair, then, that a live version for the Hippodrome in the US filmed for TV is marred by the bizarre dancing of a troupe of girls wafting feather boas like football scarves. The Zombies themselves, however, are impassive and super cool regardless of this.

'The Way I Feel Inside' (Rod Argent)
Recorded: 10 December 1964
This might be an interesting and unusual song by itself, but this marked its third release in two years, indicating that the record company had more faith in The Zombies' older work than their current. It isn't helpful that this track can be seen as 'gimmicky' too.

The Singles 1967

You taught me language, and my profit on't
Is I know how to curse. The red plague rid you
For learning me your language!
Caliban, William Shakespeare, *The Tempest*

Goin' Out Of My Head b/w She Does Everything For Me
Personnel
Colin Blunstone: lead vocals,
Rod Argent: keyboards, backing vocals,
Chris White: bass, backing vocals
Paul Atkinson: guitar
Hugh Grundy: drums
Recorded: Kingsway Studios London, 23 October 1966
Producer: Ken Jones
UK-only Release Date: 17 March 1967
Chart placings: UK: did not chart, US: 114 (Cashbox), 110 (Billboard)

'Goin' Out Of My Head' (Teddy Randazzo, Bobby Weinstein)
This was a popular and much-covered song, but whoever's performing it, it
grates on me for some reason. I think I can trace it back to a wincingly coy
Cilla Black version. No matter what I think, The Zombies were big admirers
of this Little Anthony And The Imperials' track. They were the first band to
have a hit with 'Tears On My Pillow', their debut release in 1958.
    This was The Zombies' last Decca single and was a decisive moment.
Jones added a horn section, which wasn't what the group wanted and,
consequently, Blunstone's vocal was overpowered by it. Moreover, a song
about shyness, that was originally performed with an element of trepidation,
is made faintly ridiculous by the bombast. But The Zombies must have paid
some close attention to the lyrics as it opens with one of their borrowings:
'*Well*, I think I'm going out of my head'.
    The band's releasing two cover versions in a row suggests a lack of
confidence, especially as the B-side is cracking. Yet, once again, the single
gained approving reviews, with Derek Johnson of the *NME* noting that it was
'colourfully harmonised with a big-bash treatment'. Peter Jones in *Record
Mirror* went so far as to call it 'their best yet'. However, both reviewers
commented on how the band were covering material that had too recently
made the charts in other guises. This is the problem – by this point, The
Zombies are coming off almost as a band for hire, able to turn their hand to
anything but not quite owning it. Dodie West, also on Decca, released this
single in 1964 and just reached the Top 40, and as previously mentioned,
Cilla Black covered it as the opening track on her debut album in 1965.
Petula Clarke's sophomore album included it and Chris Montez covered it –
so there were many competing cuts.

The Zombies knew that being undermined by their producer had to be for the last time. Blunstone told Cory Graves in 2013:

> We had been through a very rough period. We'd been to the Far East and we had been very badly ripped off and there were some quite scary things that happened to us there. We came back to England and a single had been released in our absence. It was a cover of 'Going Out Of My Head' by Little Anthony And The Imperials, and the mix was absolutely atrocious. So we split from our producer, and, because of the trouble in the Far East, we split with our agent. Suddenly, we had no agent, no manager, no producer, and it seemed that there wasn't so much interest in the band.

Nevertheless, the song was in the charts for six months in the Philippines.

Argent later recalled bumping into Jimi Hendrix after this session, as the guitar maestro was there recording his debut, 'Hey Joe' – a convenient symbol for how The Zombies' current sound was going to be superseded.

'She Does Everything For Me' (Rod Argent)
Recorded: May 1966
Chart placings: UK: did not chart

Yet, The Zombies' original material was certainly keeping up, as is evident in this blistering track, which develops the fuzzier sound begun on 'Indication'. The mildly discordant opening guitar riff has a hint of The Move, and the first line, 'There is nothing to say, it's all been said', has shades of The Who in its controlled frustration. Then sweeps in the swooning chorus before a return to that nagging riff punctuated with handclaps, a detail that would become a Zombies motif. A hidden gem, this is a bridge between mid-sixties garage and the heavier rock at the end of the decade. The skilful holding of words across bars is now executed expertly after the naïve attempt in 'Woman', and the slight sitar-like tone to the guitar gives a 1960s sheen without dating it too much. Argent's vocals, quite loud in the mix, are less tremulous here and the track represents a huge leap forwards. The sudden end works well with the bent guitar note hinting at a sense of satisfaction and resolution. It really should have been the A-side. Robbie Peters cut a strong version in 1968 but had little success with it.

Friends Of Mine b/w Beechwood Park
Personnel:
Colin Blunstone: lead vocals
Rod Argent: keyboards, backing vocals
Chris White: bass, backing vocals
Paul Atkinson: guitar
Hugh Grundy: drums
Recorded: Abbey Road

Producer: The Zombies
UK-only Release Date: 23 October 1967
Chart placings: UK: did not chart, US: did not chart

'Friends Of Mine' (Chris White)

An obvious single choice, being the second poppiest song on the album (after 'I Want Her, She Wants Me'), but 'Friends Of Mine' on its own somehow lacks the gravitas it gains from the company of the other songs on *Odessey And Oracle*. Nevertheless, this is the first time that White had written both the A and B-side and it's an incredibly powerful coupling, displaying the ease with which he could oscillate between catchy tunes and more mature, reflective melodies.

'Beechwood Park' (Chris White)

Whilst 'Friends Of Mine' suffers for its lack of company, this B-side's elegant finery is enhanced by this as the harmonies are sublime and shine regardless. Blunstone explained to Rich Bennet:

> They would say to me, 'Colin, you sing to us what you think is the melody'. And usually, in the verses and bridge, that would be fine, but when we came to the chorus, I would often naturally take the top harmony (I have a high voice) without realising that was what I was doing. So what they would do was set that first, sing it four or five times until I'd got it in my brain. Then Rod would give Chris White a very simple harmony because he's got to play bass. Now, this is all very well, but it often leaves Rod with a nightmare harmony to sing around these two harmonies that we're doing. I know that people have said to me, 'We've been trying to get this harmony that you're singing, what is it!?' Because it wasn't just one person on top, one in the middle and one on the bottom – it was jumping all over the place and it gave it a unique sound. But it was because we were just starting off as kids and we had to do things the best way possible that worked for us.

'Beechwood Park' is a supreme example of the skill and beauty in their vocal arrangements.

Care Of Cell 44 b/w Maybe After He's Gone

Personnel:
Colin Blunstone: lead vocals
Rod Argent: keyboards, backing vocals
Chris White: bass, backing vocals
Paul Atkinson: guitar
Hugh Grundy: drums
Producer: The Zombies
Recorded: Abbey Road

UK Release Date: 24 November 1967
US Release Date: 20 November 1967
Chart placings: UK: did not chart, US: did not chart

'Care Of Cell 44' (Rod Argent)
This was The Zombies' first single release on their new American label, Columbia. Whilst lyrically, 'Care Of Cell 44' might seem an odd choice, its tripping melody and tingle-worthy harmonies should have caught the public's ear, but alas, no.

'Maybe After He's Gone' (Chris White)
The naïve optimism contrasts resplendently with the desperate hopefulness of 'Maybe After He's Gone', making this a superb release. Blunstone always felt, however, that the A-side couldn't fail.

Odessey And Oracle

Personnel

Colin Blunstone: lead vocals, percussion

Rod Argent: keyboards, lead vocal on 'I Want Her, She Wants Me', shared vocal on 'A Rose For Emily', 'Brief Candles' and 'Hung Up On A Dream', backing vocals

Chris White: bass, lead vocal on 'Butcher's Tale' and shared vocal on 'Brief Candles', backing vocals

Paul Atkinson: guitar, backing vocals on 'Changes'

Hugh Grundy: drums, backing vocals

Recorded: 1 June – 7 November 1967, Abbey Road and Olympic, London

Producer: Rod Argent, Chris White (Ken Jones arranged 'This Will Be Our Year')

Engineer: Geoff Emerick, Peter Vince

Release Date: 19 April 1968

Chart placings: UK: did not chart, US:: 95 (Cashbox) 98 (Billboard)

> Some oracle must rectify our knowledge.
> **Alonso, William Shakespeare,** *The Tempest*

Entering Abbey Road (Studio Three, to be precise) on 3 June, with *Sgt. Pepper's Lonely Hearts Club Band,* still echoing, The Zombies began to record not only their defining album but a defining album of the decade. Whilst The Zombies certainly had die-hard fans – many of them giants of the 1960s themselves – no one expected them to peak with a work of such unqualified elegance.

With the ending of their Decca contract and the signing of a new contract with CBS Records, The Zombies were given both a new beginning and the chance to produce themselves. However, it must have been tempting to have accepted some other offers when both The Hollies and John Lennon proffered their services. With only a £1,000 budget (in fact, White and Argent would have to pay for stereo mixes from their own funds), the band rehearsed new tracks assiduously before entering the studio. This meant arrangements were diligently worked out beforehand to ensure that there would be no disappointing playbacks – the band could realise the songs to their full. Having a limited budget also ensured that producers Argent and White had to be creative with the instruments around them, not just at Abbey Road but also when moving some sessions to Olympic Studios because of availability. Abbey Road not only gifted the glitter left in the air by The Beatles, but John Lennon's Mellotron remained and proved a boon, bestowing a gorgeous resonance to the album. Lennon discovered the Mellotron whilst producing a cover version of his 'You've Got To Hide Your Love Away' by folk group The Silkie in 1966 and promptly ordered one. It's disputed if he owned or hired it, but he certainly left it behind after Sgt. Pepper and The Zombies certainly made the most of it. The Beatles had used it on 'Tomorrow Never Knows', and most famously and prominently on 'Strawberry Fields Forever', which, like The Zombies' 'Beechwood Park', would make nostalgia sound exquisite and uncanny, but it also flavoured some tracks on *Magical Mystery Tour* too. The Mellotron itself uses tape loops to recreate the sound of woodwind, brass and stringed instruments, making it like a little orchestra – perfect for the band on a budget! Yet, it also has an ethereal warmth that later synthesisers would lack.

However, a small budget wasn't so important as Argent and White received sterling support from the engineers Geoff Emerick and Peter Vince. Atkinson told *Goldmine*:

We went into Abbey Road No.2 to record *Odessey And Oracle* as The Beatles were leaving. They'd just finished doing *Sgt. Pepper*. So we walk in and Geoff Emerick and Phil MacDonald are unplugging all these patch cables. We said, 'Wait a minute, what are you doing? Plug those back in again'. And they said, 'No, no, please. We've had six months of this. It's been driving us crazy. We want to unplug all this stuff and get back to recording normally'. I think they had six or eight four-track machines lined up against the wall of the control room, all connected by patch cables. So we made them plug them back in again and we used the same technique. So, we benefited directly from *Sgt. Pepper*.

Atkinson misremembers here: McDonald engineered on *Sgt. Pepper* but didn't engineer for The Zombies until later when working on *The Zombies Recorded Live In Concert At Metropolis Studios London* in 2012. Nevertheless, the band did find some of the techniques pioneered by *Sgt. Pepper* to be advantageous. Emerick would go on to win a Grammy for his work on *Sgt. Pepper*: just one of his innovations being the close miking of Ringo Starr's drums – Grundy's would be triple-miked for this album. Ken Townsend, also an engineer on *Sgt. Pepper*, had helped The Beatles to record on an eight-track by linking two four-tracks together and The Zombies would utilise this too. Yet, the album's debt to *Sgt. Pepper* has been overstated. Geoff Emerick explained to Richie Unterberger of *Record Collector* in 2006:

A lot of people, especially a lot of the producers – as I call them, 'not real producers' – would come in and [say], 'Can you get the same sound on these drums as you get on Ringo, and can we have the John Lennon vocal sound?' But The Zombies didn't do that. They were a step up from the run-of-the-mill bands that were coming in. 'Time Of The Season' proves that. I still remember recording that session, visually. It had a good feel on it, especially the way [Rod Argent's] playing organ on it, it's great. It's just one of those tracks that clicks from the word go.

It was rare that a band who weren't signed with EMI were allowed to record at Abbey Road. Blunstone told Rich Bennett for *Sonic Scoop* in 2015:

Ken [Jones] could be a real autocrat – he could be very strict – but when we suggested to him that it might be time to produce ourselves, he helped us to get going. And to my knowledge, it was Ken Jones who got us into Abbey Road. But how he did it, who he had to kill, I'm not quite sure!

The band were still playing live dates, but managed to craft the work for the album in about six months (albeit, the bulk being from June to August), taking it from the summer to early winter, and this passing of time is evident in the shifting moods: from the sunshine pop of 'Care Of Cell 44' to the sultriness of 'Time Of The Season', from the apricity of 'This Will Be Our Year' to the mellow mists of 'Hung Up On A Dream', the album is an odyssey through hope and despair. Whilst the title came after most of the album had been recorded, parallels with the classical idea of Odyssey are apparent. Homer's *Odyssey* is centred on five main concepts: returns, journeys, the ritual of friendships, tests of character and omens. The Zombies' *Odyssey* begins with the return of an ex-con in 'Care Of Cell 44', and continues this in the hoped-for return in 'Maybe After He's Gone'; it explores the journeys of a soldier in 'Butcher's Song', a remembered journey in 'Beechwood Park' and the journey through 'neon darkness' in 'Hung Up On A Dream'; there's the reciprocity of friendship evident in 'Friends Of Mine' and 'I Want Her, She Wants Me'; there are those found failing a test of character in 'Changes' and, in some ways, 'Butcher's Song' again (although we might say the preacher is the one failing his test); finally, there's the idea of omens and portents in 'A Rose For Emily', 'Brief Candles', 'Time Of The Season' and 'This Will be Our Year'. I'm not arguing for this interpretation entirely without an arched eyebrow, but Argent had previously been planning a career teaching literature, so it's not outrageous to consider that the classic idea of Odyssey could have subconsciously informed some of these tracks, and he and White are said to have come up with the title casually whilst running through ideas in their shared flat.

The sublime cover, with its unintentional spelling error, is almost as famous as the music within and captures its delicacy and somewhat tentative psych elements in its pastel shades. Artist Terry Quirk was a flatmate of both Argent and White's in North Finchley, but he'd also been a childhood pal of Blunstone's and was the obvious choice to take the commission. Finding inspiration in both Art Nouveau and Klaus Voorman's cover design for *The Bee Gees 1st*, Quirk went one braver and didn't show the band on the front at all, albeit, they appear on the back cover. Instead, there are cameos of Shakespeare's characters as well as post-impressionist artists. Quirk recalled sketching as Argent and White threw out some ideas: they approved of the floral look, suggested adding some figures and left Quirk to decide on this, as by that time, he knew the songs well enough to make judicious choices to represent them. His use of Shakespearean references, for example, *Romeo And Juliet*, also inspired the sleeve notes written by Argent.

However, in his notes, Argent doesn't quote these famous lovers, but instead from the half-monster and slave Caliban, a character in the comic romance *The Tempest*. The play recounts how the magician Prospero causes a shipwreck in order to punish his treacherous brother. Prospero lives on an island with his slave Caliban, his daughter Miranda and his spirit servant Ariel, but he wants to become a duke, whilst Caliban longs to escape his control. Therefore, the play is often seen as an allegory of freedom and restrictions, and perhaps slipping the shackles of both record company and producer had caused Argent, a fan of Shakespeare since his school days, to recall the play. Moreover, the play incorporates more music than any of Shakespeare's other works and has also inspired composers, including Beethoven and the Renaissance musician Robert Johnson. The quotation that Argent includes is a pertinent and insightful comment, positing that the 1960s is a brave new world, but if Argent had included the rest of the quotation, something else would have been revealed.

Be not afeard; the isle is full of noises,
Sounds and sweet airs, that give delight, and hurt not.
Sometimes a thousand twangling instruments
Will hum about mine ears; and sometime voices,
That, if I then had waked after long sleep,
Will make me sleep again: and then, in dreaming,
The clouds methought would open, and show riches
Ready to drop upon me; that, when I waked,
I cried to dream again.

In this scene, Caliban is explaining how magical music can be heard on the island and he longs to enjoy its splendour again. The idea of pining for something past is evident in The Zombies' work right from 'She's Not There' but is particularly evident on 'Hung Up On A Dream'; it's often a nostalgia for something only recently passed and this is present on the entire album, which veers from the innocent to the experienced. It's also possible that *The Tempest* inspired the enigmatic album title; Alonso, the King of Naples, says, 'Some oracle must rectify our knowledge' near the close of the play, as he wonders at the magical and transformative acts that have occurred.

Argent goes on in the liner notes to say, 'anything which is not just a copy of something else is worth listening to'. Although the album is often thrown in with 'psychedelic classics', in more ways, it's a baroque work and is also looking forward to the sounds of early prog bands. Yet, in its concise vignettes, it's also a pre-emptive strike against the looser tracks that define some of the brilliant, but sprawling albums of 1968, like *The White Album* or *Electric Ladyland*.

'Care Of Cell 44' (Rod Argent)
This is in the wistful vein of The Beach Boys' song of longing and album opener 'Wouldn't It Be Nice?'. In fact, The Zombies performed some gigs with

The Beach Boys and White has commented on his admiration for *Pet Sounds*, whilst Argent told Kourtney Jmaeff at *Perfect Sound Forever*:

> I think he (Brian Wilson) had so much fantastic invention, speed and thoroughness in the way that he put tracks together in the studio, specifically around the time of *Pet Sounds*. When you look at some of the footage of him working in the studio with the Wrecking Crew, with all those great musicians, I think it's spellbinding because it's so musical, so sure and so instant. I think he was a great producer.

Originally known as 'Prison Song', it was later retitled 'Care Of Cell 69', but for some reason, the record company objected to this... The first song Argent wrote for the album (if we don't include the throwback of 'I Want Her, She Wants Me') trips in on jaunty piano, followed by bubbling bass and Blunstone's chirpy 'Good morning to you...'. It's sweetly romantic, taking the epistolary form with one lover writing to another. Then there's the twist: he's writing to a lover who's in prison. There have been some odd responses to this track over the years, with some finding it distasteful and some making certain assumptions about the gender of the incarcerated, the conjecture being that, perhaps, this was written from a female point of view. However, Argent confirmed it is from a male perspective in the *BBC Sounds Mastertapes* series and said it's about the return of a female lover to a man. It seems some found a female prisoner difficult to accept. One wonders what crime she was guilty of, as there are hints of conflict: 'Kiss and make up and it will be so nice'. Susanna Hoff and Matthew Sweet's cover from 2006 possibly subverts this.

In the 'I could be in love with almost everyone' vibe of The Summer Of Love, even an ex-con is embraced, and this joins the rank of love songs with unexpected objects of desire, such as the Meter Maid in 'Lovely Rita'. The link with Paul McCartney doesn't end there either, as the bassline is redolent of McCartney's melodic style. It marks one of White's great moments of musicianship, as it could be argued that the dancing bass and the gleaming harmonies (the acapella moments of this looking both back to 'Sometimes' and 'The Way I Feel Inside' whilst looking ahead to 'Changes' later on the album) are the song's most beautiful details.

Interviewing Argent for *The Huff Post*, Ron Galloway enquired if the piano on this track was the one used on 'Penny Lane' – the Steinway 1905. Argent thought it probably was, commenting on the piano's 'bright' tone – this is, indeed, a gleaming track.

Therefore, it's a great opener, setting at once a resplendent, if slightly uncanny, atmosphere. It also opens with diurnal imagery before the closing, crepuscular sound of 'Time Of The Season', with a slight similarity to the tone of The Moody Blues' *Days Of Future Passed*, a band Paul Atkinson much admired.

Above: The original band members: Paul Atkinson, Colin Blunstone, Rod Argent, Chris White and Hugh Grundy. (*Alamy*)

Left: First released in 1964, 'She's Not There' was voted 99 in *Rolling Stone*'s 100 Greatest Debut Singles of All Time in 2020. (*Decca*)

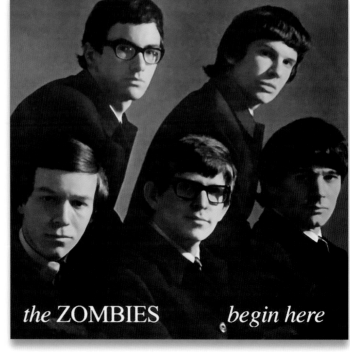

Right: The cover for the band's debut album, *Begin Here,* was photographed by Dezo Hoffman, a former photojournalist who'd been injured in the Spanish Civil War. (*Decca*)

Right: The US version of *Begin Here*, simply titled *The Zombies*, was re-released in 2003 with six bonus tracks. (*Parrot*)

MONO

THEIR U.S. DEBUT
ALBUM AS ORIGINALLY
RELEASED IN 1965

THE ZOMBIES

FEATURING
SHE'S NOT THERE
TELL HER NO

SHE'S NOT THERE • TELL HER NO • WHAT MORE CAN I DO • IT'S ALRIGHT WITH ME
YOU'VE REALLY GOT A HOLD ON ME • WOMAN • SUMMERTIME • I DON'T WANT TO KNOW
WORK 'N' PLAY • CAN'T NOBODY LOVE YOU • SOMETIMES • I'VE GOT MY MIND ON YOU
PLUS THE BONUS TRACKS YOU MAKE ME FEEL SO GOOD • LEAVE ME BE
SHE'S COMING HOME • I MUST MOVE • I WANT YOU BACK AGAIN • I LOVE YOU

DECCA

THE ZOMBIES

WHENEVER YOU'RE READY

Left: Despite a favourable review by the *NME*, this failed to chart in the UK and lingered outside the Top 100 in the US. (*Decca*)

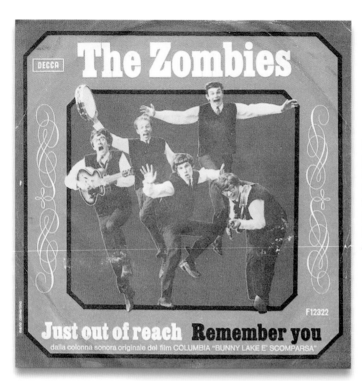

Left: Though perhaps not an obvious debt, Blunstone said he was inspired by Nina Simone's 'Wild Is The Wind' for this A-side. (*Decca*)

Right: 'Indication' marked a new sound for the band. Despite this, Decca chose an image from their first photo shoot as the cover. (*Decca*)

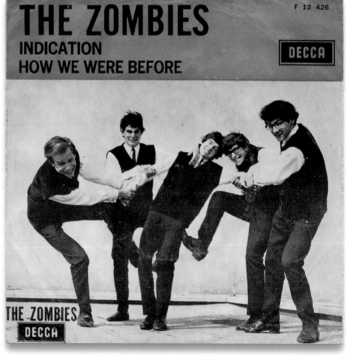

Right: Terry Quirk's intricate *Odessey And Oracle* cover art contains rock's most famous spelling error! (*CBS*)

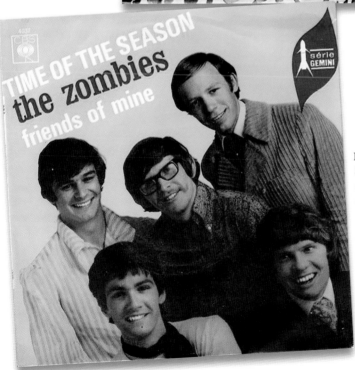

Left: 'Time Of The Season' made 35 in the *NME*'s best songs of the 1960s in 2012. (*CBS*)

Above: The Zombies despised their early promo shots, which played up their supposed academia. (*Getty Images*)

Below: The band spent Christmas of 1964 performing in Murray the K shows. (*Alamy*)

Above: In August 1964, The Zombies performed 'She's Not There' on *Top Of The Pops*. (*Pictorial Press*)

Below: The band performed 'Tell Her No' on the US show *Shindig!* in January 1965. (*ABC Photo Archives*)

THE ZOMBIES New World

Left: *New World* was released 23 years after The Zombies' 'official' final album, *Odessey And Oracle*. (*RCA*)

Right: This four-disc box set was described as 'uplifting' by Blunstone because it's such a strong testament to the band's legacy. (*Big Beat*)

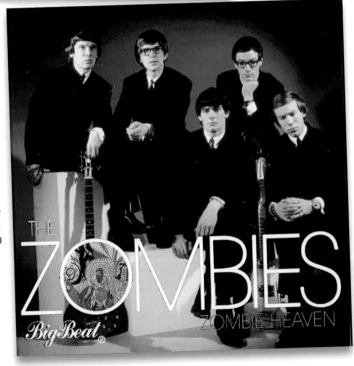

Right: This collection includes rare tracks recorded between 1964 and 1968. (*Sweet Dandelion*)

Left: The brilliant response to *Zombie Heaven* led to Argent and Blunstone recording original material again in 2002. (*Redhouse*)

Left: The first new Zombies release since 1991, the cover incorporates a snippet of *Odessey And Oracle's* artwork. (*Rhino*)

Right: This excellent compilation was billed as a 'natural sequel' to the *Zombie Heaven* box set. (*Big Beat*)

Right: For this 2015 release, the band re-recorded their fifth single, 'I Want You Back Again'. (*The End Records*)

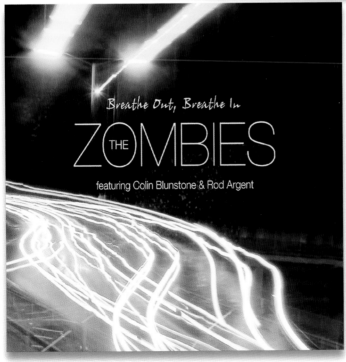

Left: The Zombies looked back to Rod's other band, Argent, and re-recorded two of their tracks for this album in 2011. (*Rhino*)

Left: Blunstone sings
The Zombies' most
famous track, 'Time Of
The Season', for a radio
broadcast in 2013.

Right: Argent is
playing the keyboard
in the same session,
a style influenced by
both classical music
and rock 'n' roll.

Left: The band performed
'This Will Be Our Year'
live from Studio 2 at
Abbey Road in 2021.

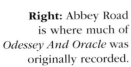

Right: Abbey Road is where much of *Odessey And Oracle* was originally recorded.

Left: In 2019, The Zombies were inducted into The Rock 'n' Roll Hall Of Fame.

Right: Chris White and Hugh Grundy joined the band for their induction performance.

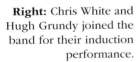

Left: This contains the live tracks from disc four of *Zombie Heaven*. (*Repertoire Records*)

Right: Unusually, this live set opens with the Blunstone solo track 'Andorra'. (*Rhino*)

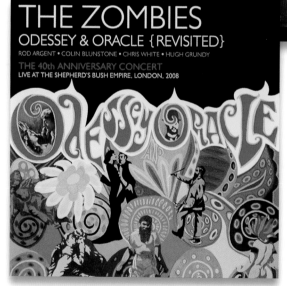

Left: The band dedicated this anniversary performance of their magnum opus to Paul Atkinson, who died in 2004. (*MVD*)

Right: Recorded in London, this double set also includes a DVD of the performance. (*Salvo*)

Left: The ten tracks on this short but powerful set work well – almost as a 'live best of'. (*Red House*)

Right: Hugh Grundy added new overdubs to 'She's Not There' for this 2002 release. (*Big Beat*)

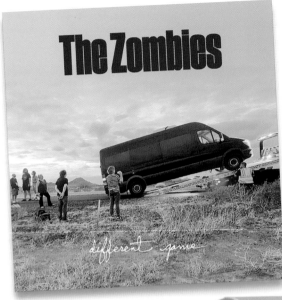

Left: Argent took advantage of the tour bus breaking down and turned the shot into their latest album cover. (*Cooking Vinyl*)

Right: A still from the 'Merry-Go-Round' video – the third single from *Different Game*.

Left: The Zombies line-up today: (L-R) Soren Koch, Rod Argent, Colin Blunstone, Tom Toomey, Steve Rodford.

Blunstone felt that this was a certain hit, but was to be proved wrong. No matter, he still re-recorded it in 1976. Dave Grohl also describes this as the song that made him want to pursue a musical career.

'A Rose For Emily' (Rod Argent)

The exquisite 'A Rose For Emily' is often compared to 'Eleanor Rigby' in its portrayal of a lonely spinster, but 'She's Leaving Home' is also a relevant reference, as it's a song of the older generation being left behind: 'There's loving everywhere but none for you', seeming to refer to the Summer Of Love itself. Emily is an isolated woman who grows roses but is never given this gift herself, and this might be one of the most beautifully compassionate songs pop has ever produced. Argent and White's vignettes aren't sneering in the manner of Dylan or Lennon, but have the solicitude of McCartney.

Another song with a similarly ironic but empathetic image of growth, but also decay, is Del Shannon's melancholic ballad 'Silver Birch' from 1968's *The Further Adventures of Charles Westover*, in which he tells the story of a jilted woman who takes her daughter to show her the symbol of heartbreak:

She takes her to the carved initials
On the silver birch
And she stands alone just like the birch
Near the tiny church.

The Zombies had already recorded 'A Rose For Emily' before this album was released in February, but there was a mutual admiration between the band and Shannon. The Zombies had shared a bill with Shannon on Dick Clark's *Caravan Of Stars* Tour and Shannon would sometimes join them on dates in England to play his hit 'Runaway', as well as the band's 'Tell Her No', which he covered himself in 1975. Chris White told Greg Russo that he enjoyed Shannon's company and was impressed by his collection of multi-coloured condoms, which he'd happily show to the band!

Returning to more sombre matters, 'A Rose For Emily' was partly inspired by the title of William Faulkner's short story from 1930. The plot involves Emily murdering her suitor so that she can keep him with her forever, even sleeping beside his corpse. There's a misconception that the song was based on the narrative itself, but Argent has said he took the title as his own starting point. 'A Rose For Emily' has been used for the podcast S-Town, a piece of investigative journalism about the South, and this seems to have solidified the idea that the lyrics recount Faulkner's scenario. Alexis Petridis, writing for *The Guardian* in 2017, said:

If you didn't know your Faulkner, you would never guess 'A Rose For Emily' was based on a story set in Mississippi. In The Zombies' hands, the titular heroine sounds like an Eleanor Rigby-ish spinster pining away somewhere in the British suburbs, a spiritual sister of downtrodden Sylvilla in The Kinks' 'Two Sisters' or the BO-afflicted lady hymned in The Who's 'Odorono'.

In reality, the narrative in the song owes little to Faulkner's tale, which also explores wealth, status, obligation and honour, etc., but takes the idea of a rose being the opposite of an elegy – it symbolises how Argent's Emily *won't* be talked about in life or death, unlike Faulkner's Emily, who is the focus of gossip. The comparison with The Kinks' 'Two Sisters' is pertinent, though. This track from *Something Else* in 1967 was also the B-side of 'Waterloo Sunset', and is in contrast to Terry and Julie, who see the bright lights, but the sisters are locked in drudgery and don't, again demonstrating a generational gap. The allusion to Odornono from *The Who Sell Out* is wider of the mark, as there is no smirk from this storyteller. Nor is there the distaste for suburbia that is hinted at in The Monkees' 'Pleasant Valley Sunday', written by Goffin And King. The lyrics mention that Mrs Gray's 'roses are in bloom', and thereby use the rose as a symbol of smug pride in middle-class neighbourhoods. The Zombies tap into that symbolism, but less critically.

Musically, the melody has a shimmer of the elegant melancholia of Grieg's *Arietta* as found on Argent's *Classically Speaking* album from 1998, with the diminished chords tightening the tension and lending the sweet melody a slight tartness. Blunstone's voice is pure and warm, whilst Argent's choirboy days are apparent in his lustrous lines. The arrangement is effectively spare, built around the gentle piano; the alternate version with strings, which is available on the 30th-anniversary edition of *Odessey And Oracle*, threatens the delicacy, but it does foreshadow the direction that Blunstone would follow with *One Year*.

Argent recollected to the *Strangebrew* podcast that Cat Stevens was a fan of the song, and The Bangles' Susanna Hoffs cites it as a favourite in the charming Zombies *Odessey* book. Her description there is both gorgeous and perceptive: it's a song with '...textures of silk and velvet and linen'. Not only does this capture the unique sensuality of the album as a whole – the almost tangible loveliness of the vocals exemplifying this – but it also evokes the tension between the old and young in the lyrics, with the Love Generation's flamboyance against the simpler beauty of Emily in linen.

'Maybe After He's Gone' (Chris White)
The first White composition on the album, this track was recorded at Olympic Studios, as Abbey Road was unavailable. The band had recorded there in their earlier days and the song does look back to previous work in its shift from minor to major chords. Yet, this shift, unusually, now points to a moment of hope, possibly misguided, being used for a different effect than the dramatic upsurge in 'She's Not There'.

This track was criticised by Ian McDonald, who pointed out its similarity to Debussy's *Jardins Sous la Pluie* ('Gardens in the Rain' taken from

Estampes – Prints from 1903 – a collection of solo piano pieces). Certainly, the gentler second part, where the rain is suspended, hints at the holding-breath quality of the lyrics before the hopeful flourish, as it seems the rain has slowed. The piece is also characterised by a lilt from the minor to the major.

In keeping with the idea of futility, the track's first title was 'One Day I'll Say Goodbye' and the home demo is collected on *Zombie Heaven*. In this version, the singer hopes to rid himself of a lover who has jilted him in the past, and it functions as a reverse of 'She's Not There' with the hope of escape. However, this premise promises more than the lyrics deliver, with the stumbling, clumsy opening verse of the demo revealing:

As blind as love made me
You can see, I am not too bright
The light I saw in her eyes
Was just greed there was no love

The re-worked lyrics below are skilfully bittersweet, with one of the loveliest opening verses of their oeuvre:

She told me she loved me
With words as soft as morning rain
But the light that fell upon me
Turned to shadow when he came...

Despite this, the singer remains optimistic, but the arrangement flickers between hope and despair constantly. The piano is sharp and almost admonishing in its staccato tone, bashing out a cowbell-like dogged rhythm in the chorus, and juxtaposes the airy harmonies. As the first track on the album, which gives prominence to the guitar, it has a more solid atmosphere, something unyielding, which suggests that the singer is doomed. There's a pun in the chords also, with a suspended chord after the phrase 'Maybe after he's gone...' indicating the agonised anticipation. The glissando that announces the song has already foreshadowed disappointment and its sadness haunts the track. Moreover, Grundy's drums are exceptionally expressive, with Greg Russo recounting, 'During the verses, echo was placed on drum rolls before the final bridge. Finally, choruses with and without drums perfectly set up overlapping acapella vocals at the end'. The echo gives the beats a shimmer, like the lovelorn heart beating, but the tolling piano notes lack this, as they're used more as percussion in some ways than the drums are, creating a tension again between optimism and pessimism. The acapella ending is another throwback to the Decca days, reminding us of another track where the singer tries to carry on regardless: 'The Way I Feel Inside'.

'Beechwood Park' (Chris White)

Having written the majority of the songs on the album, White's works haunt the atmosphere of *Odessey And Oracle* the most. But none more than 'Beechwood Park' with its innocence recollected in experience. 'Your summer world' is under threat throughout the album, whether that be by lost love, lost ambition or lost peace. The song begins in the second person with one of the most evocative opening verses in pop, a revival of 'Maybe After He's Gone' both melodically and lyrically:

Do you remember summer days
Just after summer rain
When the air was damp and warm
In the green of country lanes

The direct address takes us strolling through the park before the move to the inclusive address:

And we would count the evening stars
As the day grew dark
In Beechwood Park

The structure is intriguing as there's almost a chorus but not quite, as if the singer can't bear to disturb the dreamy mood. The bridge functions more as a chorus, with the rising and falling melody too gentle to stir the reverie. The myriad seventh chords keep tugging at the listener, creating a delicious tension, a feeling of wanting to return and a relief in the imagery of the past.

Similar to 'Strawberry Fields Forever', White looked back to a beloved place of his childhood and was inspired by the grounds of a girls' school where he used to walk and also where his grocer dad delivered shopping. Beechwood Park itself, however, was unhappy to be immortalised in song and complained!

However, White was far from home and in the Philippines when he composed this track on the piano. Recorded at Olympic rather than Abbey Road, The Beatles still proved some inspiration as Atkinson uses a Leslie Speaker Cabinet on his guitar. It had been Geoff Emerick's suggestion to use one when John Lennon was recording the vocals for 'Tomorrow Never Knows', although they had used one previously for the glimmering guitar sound on 'It's Only Love'. This shimmering effect is captured by Atkinson and hints at a panoramic view of the landscape, whilst Argent's organ susurrates behind like a breeze. The song is often described as sad in reviews, but, really, has a triumphant air, albeit triumphant like the copper tones of autumn, beautiful in its decline.

Ian McDonald scathingly pointed out the various derivations for the tracks on *Odessey And Oracle* in his review of *Zombie Heaven*, bemoaning its lack of originality. Remarking on how this track and 'Maybe After He's Gone' are reminiscent of Debussy's *Jardins Sous La Pluie*, this is undeniable. However, the impressionistic piece, with its rushing notes blurring like raindrops, is a gorgeous reference for this track in particular. McDonald might be disparaging of The Zombies being 'ersatz', but Debussy himself based his piece on folk melodies from France. And so the wheel turns ... But White merges an impressionistic composer with the late Baroque of Bach, who seemed to be a favourite of many 1960s bands, as Procul Harum's 'A Whiter Shade Of Pale' and Rupert's People's 'Reflections Of Charles Brown' attests. White's influences might be obvious, but he creates something glorious from them. You can almost smell the petrichor!

'Brief Candles' (Chris White)

This fragile song has the atmosphere of Elgar's *Chanson de Matin*, which Argent would recreate on his *Classically Speaking* album. However, this is a White composition which owes its title to a collection of short stories by Aldous Huxley from 1930. Lenny Kaye noted the influence of literature on the band, describing them insightfully as 'liter-auteurs, telling tales from inside an English prism'. Although, here, it's not just an English landscape being explored, as each verse is a vignette resembling an Edward Hopper painting depicting lonely people hunched over their drinks. In keeping with the shifts in focus, each of The Zombies' (however brief) vocalists take a turn, with Argent having the first vocal before White and finally Blunstone. The short, abrupt piano notes mimic the brief candles themselves and the vocals are as gentle as a single flame, while the chorus is almost anthemic, lending a bittersweet quality. Grundy described this as his favourite track to drum on from the album – he told People: 'I give it really good stick!'

Huxley borrowed the title himself from Shakespeare's *Macbeth*, giving *Odessey And Oracle* its second link to the Bard. Although Huxley and White use the metaphor to signify memory, Huxley's use is nihilistic, particularly in the first short story in the collection, 'Chawdron': 'Out, out brief candle! Life's but a walking shadow, a poor player that struts and frets his hour upon the stage and then is heard no more: it is a tale told by an idiot, full of sound and fury, signifying nothing'. Meanwhile, *Odessey And Oracle* is full of sound and glory...

'Hung Up On A Dream' (Rod Argent)

There's something indefinably beautiful about this track and it's probably my favourite song that isn't by either The Beatles or David Bowie! Therefore, I'm unlikely to be objective about it ...

However, it has divided admirers of *Odessey And Oracle*, as some see it as the most dated, and even tokenistic track because of its ostensibly mid-sixties imagery. Argent himself has been lukewarm about it, remarking, 'It has a line about men with flowers in their hair that makes me cringe and I really wish I hadn't written it. But, then it was the flower power era'. Also, it's been played live rarely, allegedly because of its complexities, but perhaps because its writer isn't as admiring as both Blunstone and Atkinson were, as they voted it a highlight of the album.

Whilst the flower imagery might seem to be echoing the clichés of The Summer Of Love, the epiphany in the lyrics, inspired by looking anew at a crowd, may have a more literary root. Argent's love of literature has been a constant, with him telling Johansen of his esteem for Henry Miller, Keats, Shelley and Shakespeare. Of Shakespeare, Argent said, 'The language spoke to me. It had an indefinable spiritual quality'. The same could be said about this track. However, it may be American modernism that was the source of the lyrics. Let's compare ...

Well, I remember yesterday
Just drifting slowly through a crowded street
With neon darkness shimmering through the haze
A sea of faces rippling in the heat.

...with Ezra Pound's short poem 'In A Station Of The Metro':

The apparition of these faces in the crowd:
Petals on a wet, black bough.

Whilst Pound's 1913 Imagist poem is famous for not using verbs, and Argent uses many, creating a semantic field of gentle movement, the works are similar in taking the Modernist idea of being inspired by the urban. Argent refers to streets and neon lighting, whilst Pound builds on the classic industrial symbol, travel by rail. In mechanised settings, both speakers are astounded by the sudden return to something organic and unexpectedly beautiful. They both juxtapose the ethereal with the corporeal and mundane. When Pound recollected how he'd been galvanised to write the poem in *TP Weekly*, he explained, that an experience in the Paris Underground had been the cause: 'All that day I tried to find words for what this made me feel ... I could get nothing but spots of colour'. This looks ahead to the psychedelic experience that many later 1960s tracks explore. Also, Argent's song has a sudden and potent beauty that lingers long, like this brief poem. Argent has denied that any direct hallucinogenic inspiration was behind the track, although indirect ones might be apparent, with both the phrases 'turned on' and 'it blew my mind' trailing 'A Day In The Life'. Whilst 'A Day In The Life' is not as celebratory as 'Hung Up On A Dream', each song is about observing the world around them. Perhaps the mood of Argent's lyrics takes more from McCartney's section of the *Sgt. Pepper* track, with his 'Somebody spoke and I went into a dream...'. But the lyrical inspiration probably harks back further, opening with that conversational 'Well, I remember yesterday' that they'd used regularly before.

Beginning with a low piano note or two that has a glow of 'Brief Candles', it then lifts into a partly gospel, partly impressionist rippling à la Debussy. After each line of the lyrics, the drums follow on like a trailing ellipsis, pulling the listener along with the experience. In keeping with this, the musical textures are especially rich, as Atkinson's guitar solo is gorgeously sonorous. The sweetness of the melody is given a glint here and there with the use of 9th chords. This song is often billed as psychedelic – but it transcends this label. Admittedly, there's some treatment and ethereal backing vocals, but it's hard to argue that *Odessey And Oracle* is an out-and-out psych album. The songs rely more on melody and the organic sound of the piano than on phasing, panning or passages of backmasking. As for being mind-expanding, Argent might be celebrating the purity of 1960s idealism, but as he's already reflecting fondly on a past barely passed, there's both an acceptance of the decade's epiphany regarding love and a rejection of its naivety.

Whilst the lyrics have been explored in some detail, an earlier song also informs its imagery. Simon And Garfunkel's 'Sound Of Silence' from 1964 recalls a neon-lit dream (compare this to 'Hung Up On A Dream's 'With neon darkness shimmering through the haze'), but the real subject of Paul Simon's song remains elusive, with some arguing it commented on the assassination of Kennedy. 'Hung Up On A Dream', with its being aware of 'sounds unheard', is a kind of reversal of this imagery, finding that the early 1960s might have been overshadowed by silent and oppressed voices, but by the close of the decade, more were being heard.

'Changes' (Chris White)

In some ways, this is a rags-to-riches song in the vein of Peter Sarstedt's 'Where Do You Go To My Lovely?' or Bob Dylan's 'Just Like A Woman', (a subset of 1960s songs with The Rolling Stones joining in too), but without the rancour, or indeed, misogynistic edge. The singer grieves how the woman's natural gifts have been subsumed by artifice and materials, and there's a sense of regret rather than resentment. The song sounds like a madrigal and doesn't feature any drums except bongos, although Grundy does get to sing on the track; he's joined by the rest of the band, including Atkinson.

Originally entitled 'Changes Etc.', it was the last track to be recorded for the album. The mournful organ on the chorus has an organic effect, whilst the verse is more stripped back and 'modern' to reflect the lyrics. Argent told John Wilson: 'I think that (on) a lot of the album, a lot of the songs were about colour. In something like 'Changes', we were aware of colour all the way through. So we would start with mellotron'. The flute effect of the mellotron opens the track, signifying 'And spring her voice' before there's tension created in the use of a suspended chord when the song laments 'autumn sad'. Argent explained to Chris Welch how he was influenced by the jazz chords in Cream's 'I Feel Free' when he arranged his keyboard part. Cream's track also makes use of acappella passages. Not only does the track look back slightly to Cream's second single but also to those of The Zombies themselves, being repetitive in the most winning way like some of their earlier songs.

Canada's Zumpano covered it for *The World Of The Zombies* tribute album (which also shared a name with a 1970s Zombies compilation), adding a jazzier backing. It makes for a more pleasing variant than The Chrysanthemums' reggaeish take, although I do enjoy the sudden freak-out at the end of that one.

'I Want Her, She Wants Me' (Rod Argent)

This was first recorded by the Manchester band The Mindbenders. To Argent's dismay, the group changed the chords, dropping the lurch here and there of a diminished and ruining its baroque atmosphere. The Mindbenders' version also suffers from an undistinguished vocal and unsurprisingly failed to chart. It was collected on their album *With Woman In Mind* from 1967.

Argent sings the lead on The Zombies' take and it was the first track recorded for the album. Whilst a pleasing listen, it's a little on the repetitive side, showing that it's an earlier composition than the rest, and the sudden drop to a fade-out suggests that the band were aware of this, too. It begins with an impatient rumble and then the bass drives the track, before the fade out has a hint of the baroque triumph of 'Penny Lane'. The backing vocals are like rays of sun pouring behind Argent's lead, and whilst not the most compelling track here, it's still delightful.

'This Will Be Our Year' (Chris White)

This follows on perfectly from the previous track with its carefree honky tonk piano and the sense of a fanfare in the horns, which were arranged by Ken Jones at White's request. An optimistic song, this is reflected in the chords: 'and I won't forget/the way you held me up when I was down' runs from major to minor and back to the major for 'up', making this a beautifully balanced melody. The tension between looking to a better future, but still acknowledging how the past has been rocky, is evident in its first title: 'Took A Long Time To Come'.

This has proved a popular song for more recent cover versions, with The Foo Fighters' performance being charming and understated. The Model Rockets add overdriven guitars, which work surprisingly well on the delicate melody and a more Lennon-ish vocal gives it a shiver of cynicism.

The alternate version with Argent on vocals is worth listening to, as his vocal gives it another flavour, and later live versions push the track's bluesier edge, with the harpsichord being replaced by a piano – it makes for an interesting variation.

'Butcher's Tale (Western Front 1914)' (Chris White)

White found the distinctive harmonium that characterises his anthem for doomed youth, in a junk shop, and this gives the arrangement a rasping, effortful quality, incisively evoking the attrition of the trenches and also implying a gas attack. Recounting the experience of a young butcher who is coerced into becoming a WW1 soldier, it builds on the dying as cattle metaphor of Wilfred Owen. White had initially called it the historically accurate 'Butcher's Tale (Western Front 1916)', but this was changed when the label was pressed. The track is an arresting moment on both the album and the live shows that recreated the whole work. Yet, astonishingly, White described it to *Goldmine* as 'a throwaway track, really!' It's a striking and memorable piece for many reasons.

White also revealed that The Bee Gees' debut American single from 1967, 'New York Mining Disaster 1941', had followed in The Zombies' footsteps by employing the dramatic monologue and using dates in the title. Ironically, whilst The Bee Gees were appealing to American culture (albeit in a round-about way – the Aberfan disaster in Wales was the initial impetus for the song, even though there had been a mining accident in New York in 1939) in order to establish themselves on the other side of the pond, The Zombies were looking for success on native soil, and even though the track references France, its imagery is rooted in English parochialism. Both songs are also notable for not referring directly to the title phrase in their lyrics, a notable shift from the literal titles of The Zombies' early days. Furthermore, both tracks use suspended chords sparingly at moments of tension and to intensify images of danger.

However, despite these similarities, this is still an original song with an incisive lyric. The abrupt 'Sermon' to introduce the hypocrisy of the Church is potent and sounds like a summon, enhancing the feeling of pressure on the boy. The amplification from his shaking hands to arms to, finally, a shaking mind is powerful, making physical and psychological harm one and the same. White sings this track himself, feeling his voice was more trembly to complement this imagery. Engineer Peter Vince helped to thin out White's vocal further, heightening the tremulous tone.

Opening with the shrill, demented wail that Owen referenced in his war poetry, it takes a sample of 20th-century French composer Pierre Boulez's music and plays it backwards to create its uncanny and muddy ambience. Coincidentally, Boulez had begun composing by basing his pieces on the poetry of Rilke and Baudelaire, and there's an argument that this song is based on the Great War poets, in a way. Jon Savage described it succinctly for *The Guardian* in 2011: 'Butcher's Tale' is the record's dark heart. The one stark moment of experience that makes the happiness expressed elsewhere even more delightful'.

It was released as a single in the US with the lyrics printed on it, being seen as a protest against the Vietnam War, but White has explained that he was mostly inspired by the historian AJP Taylor's writing about WW1, albeit Taylor was an outspoken critic of America's involvement in the Vietnamese conflict too. White was also affected by his uncle, who'd been killed at the Somme, aged just 16. White told Tom Preston at *Know Your Bass Player* how his mother recollected her brother *ironing out* the maggots from his uniform …

They Might Be Giants and John Wilkes Booze have covered the track, and of course, The Chrysanthemums, who turned it into a jagged punk song. However, White performing it with just Argent on piano for *BBC Sounds Mastertapes* in 2012 is incredibly moving. The most unusual cover, though, is by The Teardrop Explodes, as this track also has the fortune of being a ghost cover – their *Wilder* album from 1981 lists it on the insert, but it doesn't appear on the record itself.

'Friends Of Mine' (Chris White)

Confessing to Claes Joahnasen, White said this song was 'a bit twee'. White is being too harsh on himself, as it's a ray of sunshine power pop. In addition, it's an airy track perfectly placed to restore the equilibrium after 'Butcher's Tale' has wrenched the calm apart.

The unrestrained cymbals that splash on the bridge keep the arrangement from being too frothy and the lyrics might also have a slight bite, as this is another song about someone looking on the love of others; whilst being full of joy for them, it suggests a bittersweet, vicarious experience. Disappointment is latent in 'Hung Up On A Dream', and 'Maybe After He's Gone' and 'Care of Cell 44' are hopeful and desirous rather than actual and fulfilled after all, so even the lightest moments have shade on this album. Some have argued this track is satirically bubble-gum with a dismissive 'Ahh' from Blunstone at the end. Yet, Blunstone and White have mentioned how the singer simply lost his breath at the close. Whether sincere or arch, the cheery melody is hard to resist and does make the listener feel joy for those listed and blessed in the litany of the chorus. Amongst them is Jean and Jim, which refers to Jim Rodford and his wife, whose son Steve would go on to drum for the latter version of the band.

'Time Of The Season' (Rod Argent)

The contested line, 'Who's your daddy', is actually looking back at 'Summertime', being a nod to the song's influence here, but also across The Zombies' oeuvre. However, it has an unfortunate association, as it's a way to refer to a hooker's pimp! This slightly naughty nuance makes this track one of the sultriest and most mature by the band. Inspired by a misheard line in 'The Tracks of My Tears', which The Zombies had occasionally performed live, the singer exhorts his would-be lover to 'give it to me easy'. The steamy imagery also blends with a biblical reference, taking the symbolism of seasons from Ecclesiastes 3, which had inspired 'Turn! Turn! Turn!' with its line 'For everything there is a season'. Here, the track completes the journey from innocence to experience and takes us from the dawn of 'Care Of Cell 44' to the twilight.

Opening with a riff reminiscent of 'Stand By Me', it acknowledges the influence of Motown girl groups in its handclaps, fattened by reverb. The accentuated offbeat augments a humid atmosphere, with the bass purring beneath. Whilst this is one of the simplest tracks on the album regarding its chord structure, the simplicity is balanced with some sophisticated flourishes. The song is notable for holding back the chorus, and then the backing drops for a second, indicating that the season is all too brief, something of a tease. The solo on the coda is actually comprised of two different solos being played simultaneously, creating a type of parallel motion – a technique used by impressionist composers, here imbuing a sense of impatience and euphoria at the same time. Not surprisingly, these details made for an immensely appealing track and it scored the band a second US number one and their first in Canada.

However, it was one of the trickiest to record and caused a rare moment of disharmony in the band. Blunstone told Cory Graves about its composition:

And I was still struggling to really know the melody, to really understand the melody. Therefore, while I was standing in the studio, Rod was in the control booth saying through the callback, 'No, the melody doesn't go quite like that, it's slightly different'. And this went on for a few minutes. We had no budget, really, and we were really under pressure in the studio and it was getting more and more tense. It ended up with me saying to him something along the lines of – and with some very colourful language – 'Listen, if you know this melody so well, you come in here and you sing it'. And he said to me, 'You're the lead singer in this band! You stand there until you get it right!' It was getting quite tense. In the end, I think the sort of ironic twist to this is that when I'm singing about the time of the season for loving, Rod and I were having quite an acrimonious argument. But, I must say, I'm really glad that I did stand there until I got it right.

Being the second most covered song by The Zombies, behind 'She's Not There' of course, there's a wealth of alternatives to choose from: Michigan's The Thyme covered it in 1968 with a preppy vocal by Ralph Cole, highlighting how perfect Blunstone's voice is for the song. The clumsy increase in tempo doesn't help, but the guitar solo towards the end by Steve Vandenberg is an interesting variation. It also appears instrumentally and inessentially on *Switched On Rock* by Moog Machine, an album of Moog music inspired by Wendy Carlos' *Switched On Bach*. Billy Vaugh's James Last-style performance, also from 1969, slows the rhythm to a crawl. The Today People also slowed it down for a dull run-through, but the trumpet solo at the close is quite a promising detail, showing a lost opportunity to do something different with what had become an instant classic. Conversely, US proggers Madrigal sped it up for their 1972 attempt, but it adds nothing except showing that the rhythm is as much an integral part of the song as Blunstone's smooth delivery.

The track also birthed two Argent cuts, with White being inspired to pen 'Hold Your Head Up' after seeing the eponymous band jamming live on this track. Russ Ballard would reference it in his early Argent song 'Schoolgirl' in the driving riff, offbeat claps and lyrics of sexual awakening. Jim Rodford told Palalo: 'I do remember Russ thinking about 'Time Of The Season' when we recorded 'Schoolgirl', not to reproduce it, but to reproduce that vibe. He loved The Zombies and he liked to get it a bit ethereal. So that song was reminiscent of a Zombies rhythm track'.

Now part of popular culture, particularly in the US, the song has turned up on the soundtrack to beloved shows from *Friends* to *The Simpsons* to *South Park*. My favourite is when the vampire leader, The Baron, sings it in a New York karaoke bar in *What We Do in The Shadows*. Eminem also sampled the track for his 'Rhyme Or Reason'.

For a band who hadn't had a hit for the best part of two years, it reminded their American audience and their peers of exactly why the band had endured. In an interview with Ken Sharp for *Rock Cellar Magazine* in 2019, White recollected: 'I met Jimi Hendrix years ago when I was touring with Argent in Beverly Hills at Eric Burdon's launch of his group, War. I was standing at the bar with him and he said, "Oh yes, you did that song 'Time Of The Season'", and then he started singing it to me'.

Single Releases From Odessey And Oracle
Time Of The Season b/w I'll Call You Mine
UK Release Date: 4 May 1968 US Release Date: 5 June 1968

'Time Of The Season'
Chart placings: US: 1 (Cashbox), 3 (Billboard)
This would be re-released in December 1968, backed with 'Friends Of Mine' in the US.

'I'll Call You Mine' (Chris White)
Recorded May 1966 and December 1968
Chart Places: did not chart
This was The Zombies' first release on the Date label, which was an offshoot of Columbia. It would be collected on *Time Of The Zombies*. Being reviewed by Ken Barnes for Phonograph Records, he commented that it was a fine song, but had 'a disconcertingly beefy Blunstone vocal'. He's wrong! However, Barnes redeems himself by summing up its parent collection as 'a thrilling, magical record full of undiscovered gems and familiar classics'. He's right.

Conclusion
It seemed like this album couldn't fail to achieve the attention it merited. Regrettably, it went mostly ignored in the UK and it looked set to be the same in the US. Blunstone told Gary Ryan at the *NME* in 2021:

Apart from the DJ Kenny Everett playing tracks off it, *Odessey And Oracle* was ignored when it came out in the UK and nearly wasn't released in America. Al Kooper forced its release on his first day working at CBS [Records] as their star producer. He went to see [label boss] Clive Davis and told him: 'Whatever it costs, we have to get this album *Odessey And Oracle*. Clive told him they already owned it but weren't going to release it.

Kooper had heard the album on a holiday to England and so The Zombies were on the receiving end of one of music's luckiest breaks.

Odessey And Oracle is often catalogued as a psychedelic classic, but that's not that accurate. In some ways, it's a very natural-sounding album, with much of its atmosphere created by acoustic piano. There's no real sense of otherworldliness in the music, but rather, exquisite and intricate miniatures of real life. Al Kooper describes the songs best 'as warm melodic tapestries'.

Whilst the tracks are all strong, with many being excellent, there's an atmosphere, something indefinable about what they build together. The Chrysanthemums were so admiring of the album that they would re-record the entire work in 1992: a fascinating listen, although there are hits and misses, with the synthesisers on 'A Rose For Emily' being particularly jarring. But the album didn't need to be brought up to date, as it became more popular year on year. Paul Weller cannily commented in *The 'Odessey': The Zombies In Words And Images* that the record 'will last forever'.

There are, of course, those who demur. Ian McDonald, writing for *Uncut* in 1997, complained that:

O *And* O was primarily – and fatally – influenced by *Pet Sounds*. However obtuse many of Ken Jones's choices, he at least kept The Zombies from getting precious. Brian Wilson's choral arrangements, however, encouraged a suppressed choirboy tendency in the now self-produced group, provoking an album not only synthetic in content but prim, not to say wet, in style.

He then goes on to note which songs are derivative of other 1960s tracks or of pieces of classical music, but being fair, this sort of attack can be applied to many, many songs, and many, many artworks in general. This can often be quite a pleasure, especially for we anoraks, but if done mean-spiritedly, it is unfair, as we could apply this kind of criticism to The Beatles too...

Odessey And Oracle is one of the finest examples of the peaks that great songwriting can reach. If Keats had been in a 1960s British Invasion band, he'd have recorded something like *Odessey And Oracle* (incidentally, Blunstone would later be a member of the band Keats, a spin-off of The Alan Parsons Project, who'd release one eponymous album in 1984).

The legend goes that the 'failure' of the *Odessey And Oracle* album is inconceivable. Yet, it seems the curse of *Begin Here* was potent again:

the album just missed being released at the right time. If we consider the Dionysian feel of 1968 after the sunshine of The Summer Of Love, as exemplified by *Beggar's Banquet, Electric Ladyland* and the darker corners of *The White Album*, the bucolic splendour of the collection is admittedly out of place. It has more in common with that other lost masterpiece, The Kinks' *Village Green Preservation Society*, which emerged late in 1968 but is similarly nostalgic for a recent but threatened heritage. There's some insight in a review from the early 1970s, which, whilst being mistaken, reveals a difficulty with *Odessey and Oracle*. US critic and, later, singer with the punk band Angry Samoans, Metal Mike Saunders, when writing for *Fusion* in 1972, remarked:

> I've never liked that album – 'Time Of The Season' and 'Friends Of Mine' are great, and 'Care Of Cell 44' is good, but the rest of the LP suffers largely from the common post-*Sgt. Pepper* maladies of 1968. Namely, it doesn't rock. And if it doesn't pass as rock, why, what is it? Don't ask me, but I sure was glad to see that era end. When you get to 'Friends Of Mine' and 'Time Of The Season' at the close of *Odessey And Oracle*, they stand out just by being simple, unpretentious rock.

The album defies categorisation unless we plump for the bathetic term pop. It's also clear that the design of the album has some lazy links to *Sgt. Pepper,* even though the music has its own identity. It's curious that the standouts for this reviewer are the most commercial, showing that The Zombies couldn't win! There wasn't much of an audience for their more experimental work and the pop market proved capricious. Saunders continued by lamenting White's 'decline': 'Chris White's songwriting on that last Zombies release evidences a severe deterioration compared to his earlier work'. We'll move on ...

But the band weren't considering its legacy, as in the immediate aftermath of the album, they split up. White told Russo that regardless of the album's destiny, it was going to be the band's ultimate work:

> That was the last straw. Basically, the record company didn't like it and wasn't planning on putting it out. It was actually after the recording of the album that Hugh, Colin and Paul basically said that they couldn't survive on what the group was making. It wasn't enough: 'How do we eat?' Rod and I didn't lose and wanted to continue in the record business.

Blunstone elaborated to *Goldmine*:

> I remember the actual words that were spoken. We were rehearsing acoustically at Chris White's flat in Finchley. I think everyone was tired and being a bit negative and actually, as I remember it, Paul said, 'Well, I think it's time for me now, I think that's enough'. And Rod said, 'If Paul's going to

leave, I think we should fold the band'. And no one argued. I just think we were all very, very tired. It was remarkably undemonstrative, probably very English. After all those years and those miles of travelling and everything.

With the album being a studio work, in the long run, it has endured, but in the short term, it further sealed their demise, as it was difficult to reproduce the songs at gigs, particularly because of the Mellotron. White told *Goldmine*:

> We did 'Time Of The Season' and a few things like that. We tried 'A Rose For Emily'. The difference in those days, doing a gig in Richmond in London or something, was the fact that they just wanted to dance. So we had a mixture in our stage act of dance-type stuff and unusual jazz-based stuff, as well as material from the album.

It seemed as though there just wasn't an audience for *Odessey And Oracle* ...

Boise, Idaho, is known as The City Of Trees and it was here that The Zombies, in a sense, flourished back to life in 1969. 'Time Of The Season' was granted heavy radio play and the defunct band had their second number one and a silver disc.

But this was a curious kind of success – a band with a *Billboard* hit was nowhere to be found, so willing imposters stepped in and a number of faux Zombies roamed around the gig circuit. John Mendelsohn reviewed one of these imposter Zombies combos for *The Los Angeles Times* in 1969, observing that 'it was as repellent as it was disappointing' and that it was further brought low by 'unthinkably bad jokes and moronic patter'. Yet, it did prove that the band had an audience, nevertheless. Although those counterfeit Zombies would come back to haunt them later ...

The Singles 1969

Imagine The Swan b/w Conversation Off Floral Street

Personnel

Rod Argent: keyboards, vocal

Russ Ballard: guitar

Jim Rodford: bass

Bob Henrit: drums

Recorded: Morgan Studios, 18 December 1968

Producer: Argent/White

UK Release Date: 30 May 1969

US Release Date: 29 April 1969

Chart placings: UK: did not chart, US: 77 (Cashbox), 109 (Billboard)

'Imagine The Swan' (Rod Argent, Chris White)

The harmonium is a pretty sound, floating like a swan, but this song skirts too close to the band Marmalade in its overreaching chorus. Whilst a decent band in their own right, there's something off about The Zombies emulating Marmalade's dramatic, but simultaneously light sound. In fact, this is probably one of the most dated songs in their catalogue. However, the power that lends it a brief sense of the epic at the close is effective, and if this had been called upon sooner, it would have given it a sharper edge.

Nevertheless, it's an engaging misfire all the same, having a baroque melody inspired by Bach's 'The Well-Tempered Clavier' – the Clavier being the keyboard instrument. Bach wrote it to display all 24 keys and, indeed, this song vividly displays Argent's virtuosity, although it was written by White. Its lyrics share something with 'Changes', using colour imagery to depict a failing love: 'Well I have a picture in colour of you' dimming to 'For the colours are gone/You've become kind of grey', making this a reverse Ugly Duckling. Argent takes the lead vocal as this is recorded by an in-utero Argent, as in the band, including Russ Ballard and Bob Henrit. However, it's still credited to The Zombies because this was a kind of interim group, testing the waters to see if The Zombies could be resurrected on the back of the million-selling 'Time Of The Season'.

'Imagine The Swan' was first collected on *The Best And Rest Of The Zombies* from 1984, along with 'Girl, Help Me', 'I Could Spend The Day' and 'I'll Keep Trying'.

'Conversation Off Floral Street' (Rod Argent, Chris White)

The working title being 'Bonnie And Clyde', this is a frenetic instrumental that Argent composed as a dance piece for his girlfriend and later wife, Cathy. Cathy was a dancer in a company run by Molly Atkinson, Paul's first wife, (as in Paul and Molly from 'Friends Of Mine').

It has an apparent debt to Dave Brubeck and also nods to Keith Emerson's work with The Nice. The rise of groups with virtuoso keyboardists, including

Deep Purple, The Doors and Iron Butterfly, can be traced in some part back to The Zombies' sound in general (that is, splitting solos between the keyboards and the guitar) and, of course, Argent, in particular, who along with Alan Price, was composing songs around the piano much more than other British Invasion bands. Whilst this piece might be dispensable, it gives a hint of what Argent's next project would sound like, and it's at least a pleasing listen until the middle section, which is marred by a very Phoenix Club organ sound that jars.

It was mistakenly titled 'Conversation *Of* Floral Street' on the single pressings.

If It Don't Work Out b/w Don't Cry for Me
Personnel
Colin Blunstone: lead vocals,
Rod Argent: keyboards, backing vocals,
Chris White: bass, backing vocals
Paul Atkinson: guitar
Hugh Grundy: drums
Recorded: Decca Studios London, 8 July 1965; vocal and string overdubs at Morgan Studios, December 1968
Producer: Ken Jones, Rod Argent, Chris White
US Release Date: July 1969
Chart placings: US: did not chart

'If It Don't Work Out' (Rod Argent)
Jonathan Donaldson, writing for *Vanayaland* in 2015, described Blunstone as 'basically Dusty Springfield in drag', and Argent got a chance to write for Springfield proper when she asked him for a song after sharing a bill with the group. Coincidentally, she had been discovered by Tito Burns when she was part of The Springfields.

'If It Don't Work Out' opened the second side of *Everything's Coming Up Dusty*, released in the autumn of 1965, which also included songs by Bacharach/David and Goffin/King, allowing Argent's work to shine amongst these luminaries. Springfield gives a strong performance, wringing out every drop of the memorable chorus and improvising well on the fade-out. Nevertheless, overall, it lacks the power of The Zombies' cut, and Argent expressed regret that he wasn't able to be involved in the production of her version, as he was working on another project at the time. Springfield's vocal seems a little too high to begin with, leaving her no room to increase the drama, whilst Blunstone's vocal builds skillfully. There's something a little uneasy about the shift to the middle section, with The Zombies handling it better, having a short transitional pause that makes it smoother. It's not hard to see why some of The Zombies would have preferred to have recorded it first themselves, and there was tension when Argent revealed that the band wouldn't be. However, it was eventually released as a single, but excellent as it is, by then, it seemed too retrospective in sound, especially after 'Time Of The Season'. No matter, because the harmonies, the short stabs of strings and the minimal piano trills make for a compelling listen.

'Don't Cry For Me' (Chris White)

Whilst this doesn't stand out that much on the *R.I.P.* album, hearing it on its own emphasises its punchy sound and the excitement built by the rising intro, emboldened by thick harmonies. Although this complements a strong A-side, it might have proved a judicious first choice also.

After The First Breakup

And so The Zombies were laid to rest ... for the time being ... Yet, the erstwhile members had many other lives in between.

Argent and White continued to write together before developing into the prog group, Argent. White played on some proto-Argent songs but wanted to focus on production and songwriting, so Jim Rodford, who was between bands, was brought in on bass. White has also magnanimously commented that Rodford was the more skilled bassist, and as the music was becoming increasingly complex, he would prove crucial. Previously, Argent and White had been impressed by the musicians they'd seen playing with The Roulettes and therein found their guitarist and drummer, respectively, in Russ Ballard and Bob Henrit. They first worked on 'Girl Help Me', which was developed from 'Call Of The Night', a track that The Zombies had demoed, yet this wouldn't be under the new band's name yet as it hadn't been decided.

Nexus was considered as a band name and would grace a later album, as well as being Argent and White's production company, but it was suggested that Rod's surname would be a better moniker. Argent was reluctant at first. However, not only did it update band names like The Jimi Hendrix Experience or The Graham Bond Organisation, but it also showcased a number of other meanings, including silvery white and being French for money. Incidentally, the Argent track written by Ballard, 'It's Only Money', could be read as 'It's Only Argent'...

1970 saw their eponymous debut, an atmospheric collection opening with the sultry 'Like Honey'. There's also the pop-rock blend of the catchy 'Be Free' and 'Dance In The Smoke', with *Odessey And Oracle* flavoured melodies and harmonies, and it's the 'Time Of The Season'-esque whirling keyboards and striking rhythm that sets the pattern for the album as a whole. Richie Unterberger's review said: '[It's a] fair approximation of late-period Zombies, with a much heavier hard/progressive rock feel. There's nothing that's nearly as arresting as *Odessey And Oracle*, but it's not bad at all'. He has a point that it's not as immediately appealing, as the tracks are significantly longer and looser, and the mood is more sustained than varied, but it proved a very promising debut.

However, Ken Barnes, writing for *Phonograph Record* in July 1972, reflected:

Argent recorded an exceedingly enjoyable and infinitely promising debut album, full of short, concise, memorable ditties ('Liar', 'Like Honey', 'Free Fall' and others), with sterling vocals and any number of infectious musical riffs and hook lines; the band looked potentially capable of equalling or surpassing the achievements of the parent Zombies...

The inventive chords of The Zombies are developed even further and Argent's keyboard work is excellent. Rather than each solo simply increasing in dynamics or speed, there is a design that circles around motifs, builds, drops and often returns to the perfect moment, evincing both technical expertise and an acute sensitivity about what the track needs. Ballard's guitar work is complementary and he continues the tradition of The Zombies, where the band play cohesively rather than competitively. And Ballard would help to launch Argent in America as his 'Liar', a solid track with compelling use of dynamics, dented the US charts and was covered by Three Dog Night.

Rod Argent's favourite album, *Ring Of Hands,* followed next in 1970. Combining the heavier, humid sound of the previous album with flavours of gospel, barroom blues, soulful vocals and even a hint of funk in the rhythms, it also sprawls into true prog epics with 'Lothlorien'. And there's the brilliantly overblown 'Cast Your Spell Uranus' from Ballard, with a classic early 1970s rock verse, recounting the older predatory woman/younger man scenario (See also Rod Stewart's 'Maggie May' and 'Raped And Freezing' by Alice Cooper):

She was forty-one, I could've been her son
They call her the princess of the Moon
She had the cars, the clothes, and the scenes
I had my long hair and my jeans...

Barnes reacted differently to this work, commenting:

[*Ring Of Hands*] was ambivalent and ambiguous, teetering precariously between enthralling pop tunes along the lines of the first album ('Chained', 'Rejoice') and pretentious, overextended organ exhibitions ('Lothlorien') or dire funky blues (the dreaded near-hit 'Sweet Mary'); ultimately an unsatisfying but not entirely unhopeful affair.

However, it's a fallacy that every album was less well-received critically than the one before it. Whilst Barnes might not have thought highly of their next album, *All Together Now* from 1972, it earned praise from *Rolling Stone.* The cover looked back to 'Friends Of Mine' by gathering their nearest and dearest around them. It also has a link to Blunstone's solo career, as it includes a quartet of songs that he would incorporate on *Ennismore*; Blunstone also played support at some Argent gigs. 'Pure Love' is often billed as the weak spot, and some parts lack a strong melody, admittedly, but it does display Argent's virtuosity to its fullest, especially in the first half, inspired by Bach. The album is home to their biggest hit, 'Hold Your Head Up', with an incredible organ solo by Rick Wakeman, so it's no surprise that the album found itself ranking at 33 on *Mojo*'s 40 Cosmic Rock Albums in 2005.

In Deep followed in 1973, containing 'God Gave Rock n Roll To You' written by Ballard, which reached 18 on the UK chart and was on the outer edge of the Top 100 stateside. The album contained less memorable Argent/White compositions than previously, although 'Be Glad' is a great showcase for the whole gamut of Argent keyboard styles from the Chopin-esque to the Hammond demon. *Nexus* came the following year – based more on instrumentals, this is a divisive piece. Quite simply, if you like extended organ solos and the kind of music to soundtrack epics, it's for you. However, the split between Ballard's more rock 'n' roll orientations and Argent's improvisations was becoming apparent, and this marked Ballard's last recording with the band. The first vocal track on the album is the *fourth* song, the gentle ballad 'Love', written by Ballard. John Tobler, for *Let It Rock* in 1973, said that Blunstone had been emphatic that Argent were one of the best bands around, and after hearing *In Deep*, he had to agree with him, albeit praising Ballard's tracks more than Argent's. The same year, *Encore: Live In Concert* was released. A highlight was Ballard singing an understated 'I Don't Believe In Miracles' backed with his own piano playing. 'Time Of The Season' was also performed, of course. The band had been receiving solid notices for their live work, with Ed Jones defining the band's sound as 'heavy-rock-pop' in his mostly favourable review of the Edinburgh gig in 1973 for *Cracker*.

Their penultimate album appeared the next year. Chris Welch, for *Melody Maker* in 1974, wrote: 'The tapes he played me of their forthcoming album *Circus* seems to indicate that we can expect greatness from the team that once seemed destined to be a poll-winning ensemble, until the steam ran out'. As it happened, *Circus* received some of the most mixed reviews and marked the formation of a different line-up. John Grimaldi replaced Ballard and was a St. Albans boy from Argent's school, which was allegedly a coincidence after Argent had auditioned around 150 hopefuls. Argent told Welch: 'Russ always thinks in terms of songs, whereas I think of the way they can be arranged and developed. If you listen to Russ's new LP, you can hear they are all three-minute songs'. *Circus* was certainly not full of three-minute songs, being an ambitious recreation of The Big Top experience, and it is mostly well realised, but many tracks are of the same tempo, meaning it can fail to grip one's attention at times. *Counterpoints* was released the same year and Tony Visconti joined Argent and White for the production. This built on the funk rhythms of earlier albums and the more sprawling tracks of *Circus*, but was to be their last release. There was an unexpected change in their line-up due to illness, so some of Bob Henrit's drumming duties were taken over by Phil Collins. There was also a change in songwriters, as the album contained Jim Rodford's epic 'Time' and a short John Grimaldi composition, the gentle 'Waiting for the Yellow One', and also his jazzy instrumental 'It's Fallen Off' alongside Argent/White compositions.

Rod Argent took time after the break-up of his second band to teach himself to read music before releasing his first solo album *Moving Home*, in 1978. Later performing on Andrew Lloyd Webber's *Variations* with Clem Clempson led to further collaborations, including Argent's playing on 'Memory' from *Cats*. The early 1980s saw him producing Frida Lyngstad's 1981 LP *Something's Going On* and working with John Dankworth in 1983 on *Metro*.

Blunstone also had a connection to Webber, being asked to sing on the *Jesus Christ Superstar* album, but a record company clash prevented it. Coincidentally, Tim Rice's father had also worked at the de Havilland factory and he'd attended the same school as Argent. Blunstone might have had to pass on that opportunity, but he, too, began a varied solo career in the 1970s. This started auspiciously with the consummate *One Year* in 1971, which boasted the number 15 hit 'Say You Don't Mind'. Sonic Youth's Thurston Moor told Emily Barker for the *NME* in 2014: 'I don't think his solo music gets the recognition it deserves. In particular, 'One Year' is a gorgeous example of classic British pop music. It's very personal, very sophisticated in its sentiment'. The album loosely tracked events in his life, but Argent/White songs are also performed, including 'She Loves The Way They Love Her', 'Smokey Day' and 'Her Song'. Enhanced by some exquisite string arrangements by Chris Gunning, it's a much-admired album that, like *Odessey And Oracle*, has been rediscovered. Blunstone supported ELO in 1972, touring with a string quartet. My 14-year-old dad saw this gig with his reluctant dad, who just about managed to stand Blunstone, but was less complimentary of ELO!

Colin Larkin thought that *One Year*'s follow-up *Ennismore* was superior. There are some similar string arrangements, but it also advances the jaunty sound as set by the Mike D'abo composition 'Mary, Won't You Warm My Bed' ostensibly to make the songs easier to perform live. 'Quartet' is a highlight, evincing how Blunstone's songwriting talents burgeoned, as evident on the songs that make up the 'Quartet' in particular, some of which were co-written with drummer David Jones. Blunstone's lyrics also took a more sensuous turn, especially on 'Exclusively For You' where he croons, 'The light's turned off, but there's no woman to turn on/And there's no happiness in having to undress'. It also includes Argent/White's 'Andorra' – unsurprisingly the most Zombies of the songs. Ron Grainer had recorded a perky instrumental under this title, the B-side to the superb *Man In A Suitcase* theme, but White subverts this, recounting how the holiday can only disappoint; it has a fantastic ruminative and brooding mood:

Hey, there's a darkness
In the sky that's not the night
Hey, there's a rain cloud there
That's shutting out the light.

Journey followed in 1974 – including the Argent/White credits – 'Wonderful' and 'Beware' and White produced the album. It's enjoyable if inessential, as some of it drifts by and 'This Is Your Captain Calling' is whimsical à la 'Telescope', but jangling in this context.

1976 witnessed the release of *Planes* and then Blunstone saw the 1970s out with *Never Even Thought* and *Late Nights In Soho*. He began the 1980s with a collaboration with Dave Stewart on a cover of Jimmie Ruffin's 'What Becomes Of The Broken Hearted', and then continued to trawl through Motown's back catalogue, releasing 'Tracks Of My Tears' two years later. In the same year, he worked with The Alan Parson's Project and collaborated with them several more times and with their offshoot group, Keats. Blunstone co-wrote two of the tracks on the only Keats album, 'Tragedy' and 'Night Full of Voices', with Cockney Rebel, Pilot and sometime 10cc and APP drummer Stuart Elliot.

New World

Personnel
Colin Blunstone: lead vocals,
Rod Argent: keyboards on 'Time Of The Season'.
Chris White: bass, vocals
Paul Atkinson: guitar on 'New World'
Hugh Grundy: drums
Sebastian Santa Maria: guitar
Tim Renwick: guitar
John Woolloff: guitar
Laurie Wisefield: guitar
Duncan Browne: guitar
Claude Nobs: harmonica
Producer: The Zombies, David Richards, Chris White
UK Release Date: April 1991
Chart placings: UK: did not chart

> Oh, wonder! How many goodly creatures are there here! How beauteous
> mankind is! O brave new world, that has such people in 't!
> **Miranda, William Shakespeare, *The Tempest***

Not only were counterfeit Zombies marauding around the gig scene in the
1960s, but this continued throughout the 1970s and even beyond. White told
Greg Russo:

> We took legal action, but it didn't do much good. Whenever we'd catch up
> to one of these phoney bands, they'd have already played the gigs, made
> their money and split. They even played the Whisky A Go-Go in LA and The
> Move, where fans of ours were in the audience, and they actually threw beer
> cans at the stage yelling, 'fuck off, you're not the real Zombies!'

One of these bands, calling themselves The Original Zombies, included
future ZZ Top members Dusty Hill and Frank Beard. They didn't go as far
as some counterfeits, who claimed that Blunstone had been killed in a
car accident (a ghoulish but convenient way of explaining why the vocal
didn't sound anything like him!) but said he'd gone to jail instead, putting
a new slant on 'Care Of Cell 44'...
Blunstone would write, amusingly and strangely poignantly, of this in 'Sing
Your Own Song', which opens with 'Yesterday, in Rolling Stone, I read/A man
said I'm dead', and this was released in demo form as one of the bonus tracks
as part of *One Year*'s 2022 reissue. He told Gary Ryan in 2021:

> Nothing worked until a fan thought they were so atrocious that he went into
> their dressing room, pulled a gun on them and told them to stop performing

as The Zombies! I'm in no way suggesting that's the answer to every issue in the music industry, but in this case, it was very effective, as they were never heard of again!

The band were dismayed to find that they had to fight to claim back their name legally, as they had little power to stop the pseudo-Zombies without this. A particular indignity was an incarnation of the band that included one conveniently named Ronald Hugh Grundy, masquerading as the real drummer Hugh Grundy. Undeterred by the fact that the imposter was a bassist, he explained this anomaly by saying that the audience wanted to see an original member upfront!

Whilst it was frustrating for the band that their legacy was taking a bashing from these inferior players, it did help them reclaim their name and then record as The Zombies again. But there were still struggles ahead, as securing a record deal proved difficult; the band wanted to produce themselves, but this limited their options because companies wanted more control over the finished product. Eventually, RCA in Germany offered them a one-album deal, although they would record in England and Switzerland, which was home to guitarist and keyboardist Sebastian Santa Maria. Chris White would produce much of the album, and David Richards was also brought in and worked on 'New World', 'I Can't Be Wrong', 'Lula Lula' and 'Heaven's Gate'. Richards had previously produced Chris Rea, Iggy Pop and David Bowie, but the band's tribulations were not yet ended. Argent was reluctant to be involved in the album, and Atkinson, who did want to contribute, lived abroad and wouldn't be able to commit to the entire project. He guest stars on the lead single and title track. Therefore, the ranks had to be swelled some other way: White had previously worked with the Chilean keyboardist Sebastian Santa Maria, so his services were called upon, whilst Blunstone's one-time flatmate (in Ennsimore Gardens, inspiring the title of Blunstone's second solo album) and collaborator Duncan Browne was brought in on guitar. Browne was best known as a member of the British band Metro, and for co-writing the suggestive 'Criminal World', which would find its way onto David Bowie's smash album *Let's Dance*. Browne and Blunstone had formed Camino together in the 1970s, although this project didn't take off. Further enhancing the line-up were three other guitarists: Tim Renwick, who'd played with Junior's Eyes, Alan Parsons and Procol Harum; also, Wishbone Ash's Laurie Wisefield and The Kingpins' John Woolloff. However, Grundy, who was available after stints with Christie and then working with various record companies in A&R, was available to provide the backbeat.

Unfortunately, the financial backing in America fell through, so, ironically, it wasn't released in the country where it might have been most successful, and which had partly inspired the lead track. Yet, it was released as *The Return Of The Zombies* in Germany, and Blunstone, White and Grundy's constant presence on the album meant that this 'reunion' was certainly more legitimate than those of some bands, but it has to be said that Argent's absence is keenly apparent. Having three guitarists might have embellished some bands, but as The Zombies were never really a guitar combo, it doesn't add much here. Yet, the album did well enough to be released a year later in the UK, the title having been changed to *New World*. It's undoubtedly a new sound for the band, and there are a number of tracks certainly worth investigating.

'New World (My America)' (Andy Nye, Chris White)

Lacking the parentheses on the German release, the 'My America' was added for the UK version. Written by White with his nephew Andy Nye – who'd trained as a classical pianist, backed Leo Sayer and Barbara Dickson and written for Roger Daltry – it's an anthemic song, and an obvious choice for a lead single, although it might have benefited from getting to its victorious chorus a few bars sooner. Driven by guitars, the track demonstrates that Atkinson's tone has a sharper edge than previously and its sound is certainly of the late 1980s. However, this is the problem with the album as a whole: whilst, at the time, it might have made for a respectable updating of the band's identity, it now sounds more dated in places than their Decca recordings!

The music might be of its time, but the lyrics reference John Donne's 'His Mistress Going To Bed' from 1633 (which is acknowledged in the lyric booklet), as they recount a hopeful lover embarking on a new affair and use the same conceit of geographical discovery. Donne's poem commands:

Licence my roving hands, and let them go,
Before, behind, between, above, below.
O my America! my new-found-land.

Whilst the song's lyrics use this metaphor of travel, they don't completely take its erotic direction, but they do remind of the imagery in 'Time Of The Season': 'In this time, give it to me easy/And let me try with pleasured hands...' as Blunstone sings, 'Lost in her gentle curves/I feel her warmth/ her open hand'. Argent told Alec Palao, 'I used to like that little phrase, 'with pleasure hands', which is quite unusual and I quite like the way that it sat in that song'. It seems that White was also an admirer and it possibly sparked something here. Whilst this track might not be a classic like 'Time Of The Season', it's a sound ballad that makes for an effective opener, and it may, in turn, have inspired Rod Argent on a later Zombie album when he thanked America on 'New York' from *Still Got That Hunger*.

As an opener, it sets the atmosphere of the album, with a pattern of musing verses and swelling choruses, and an arrangement and production that remind me of 'grown up' pop in the style of Fleetwood Mac's *Tango In The Night*, for instance, but this also shows how this apparent contemporising of the band's sound was already a little behind.

'When Love Breaks Down' (Paddy McAloon)

Written by Prefab Sprout's frontman Paddy McAloon, 'When Love Breaks Down' was a hit for them in 1984, being from the *Steve McQueen* album. The record company had felt that a contemporary track would bring more listeners and its atmosphere of both fragility and resignation doesn't seem out of place with the other songs. Perhaps it was still too recent a hit to release as a single as some thought, but it's a strong performance with an effortless vocal from Blunstone, which is more controlled than McAloon's, and it would probably have dented the charts had it been released as a stand-alone too. The rippling keyboards flow gorgeously around the rueful melody, complementing some poignant (and very Chris White!) imagery of September rain, whilst a muscular bass line effectively threatens the tender imagery. White told *Goldmine*: 'We did a cover of a Prefab Sprout song, 'Love Breaks Down'. They were knocked out. I think that's the only song of theirs that had been covered'. It has since been performed by Lisa Stansfield and Snow Patrol.

'I Can't Be Wrong' (Sebastian Santa Maria)

Opening with a gentle, trickling refrain, this is too similar to the previous song and would have been better placed a track or two further on. A song pattern has already been established, with a delicate intro that grows to a swelling chorus: this can make for a safe single but becomes tedious across the album as a whole. This is, in fact, an effective song and imagining it with a simple piano backing and just the gleam of Blunstone's voice, it could have been realised more powerfully. Although a pleasing melody written by Santa Maria, it's too slight to have another anthem constructed around it. The harmonies on the chorus are smooth, but, whilst Grundy's drumming is tasteful for the most part on the album, here, it's too sibilant and sharp, striving for some 'punch the air' moments...

Curiously, this is another track that conjures up 'Time Of The Season' vibes, as it opens with, 'For me time is only seasons/And nights are simply broken days', yet, the images don't require a close inspection: 'I said the sun must be freezing/January should only be a place/I thought there was but there isn't'.

'Lula Lula' (Chris White)

Released as a single in Germany, backed with 'I Can't Be Wrong', this is unequivocally a White track and certainly a highlight of the album being a gorgeously romantic declaration of love; White said that it was actually written about 20 years before it was finally recorded and had been arranged previously with the help of Blunstone and Argent. This might also explain why it does sound genuinely like an update of The Zombies. Another guitar arrangement, it leaves one wondering how Argent's jazzy fills would have lent some tension, but the sombre melody, that somehow complements the singer's joyous discovery of love (that use of 7th chords, again, adds an almost surprised tone, but there are also rich 11ths sweetening it), is compelling, and Blunstone sings with a refined tenderness. The song recalls the more mature and reflective ballads from *A Hard Day's Night* a little in its melody and evinces how pop can 'grow up', whilst retaining a purity. The attention to detail is reminiscent of Zombies of old, as the suspended chord comes in knowingly to augment the 'Hold my hand' line, gifting a wry pun. The synth is tastefully understated and Grundy's unobtrusive drumming finds the band working beautifully together, demonstrating how The Zombies still had much to offer.

'Heaven's Gate' (Andy Nye, Chris White)

An acapella opening, with the chorus upfront, helps to change the atmosphere of the album and disrupts the pattern that was being set. This is a professional track that shows its writers undoubtedly know how to structure a song and create hooks – not surprising, as Chris White is one of them. However, it's too polished, a little anonymous, and therefore, not as memorable as the others, with the vocals too low in the mix, making for a muddy sound – yet, the propulsive riff on the fade-out is arresting. It's credible 1980s pop by numbers and might have worked better if White and Nye had offered it to a different act, although, again, Grundy's off beats are an interesting detail. The more one considers this track, it could be that it's too big for Blunstone's sensitive tones, and perhaps another member could have taken over the vocals.

Lyrically, it's another song to open with 'and': 'And now heaven's gate is open wide for you have put a light inside me', and it recounts falling in love again as a moment of arrival like the title track. However, the moment is no longer like discovering another continent on this world but is likened to ascension to Heaven instead.

'Time Of The Season' (Rod Argent)

This is a different version (and the more preferable) from the one on the original German release, as this sounds incredibly close to the original. You might say, what's the point? Of course, it won't replace it, but missing an opportunity to have four of The Zombies play on a stone-cold classic would be churlish, as would suggesting it also made the album more saleable...

It can be argued that there's a richness to the drums that adds a further warmth not on the original, and the extended solo on the fade out is definitely worth hearing too. Even after 20 years, Blunstone's control of his vocal is superb – his manipulation of the soar and swoop is impeccable and reminds one of how his voice and Argent's playing are a formidable coupling. I only wish there was more of Argent on the album ... He later explained to *Goldmine*:

It was such a perfectly formed little period that it would just be cheapening it, tarnishing it a bit, to go back and re-form. I don't feel quite that way about

Argent, even though I'm not thinking about re-forming Argent. The Zombies just felt like something that existed at a young and, sort of, important time of our lives and it's become a bit of a cult, and I just want to remember it as it was.

He would, of course, reconsider!

'Moonday Morning Dance' (Sebastian Santa Maria)

At last, a pacier track with some proggy keyboards. The chilly echo on Blunstone's voice resembles Genesis' later poppier tracks and the jittery rhythm, with chanting backing vocals, has hints of Kate Bush's 'The Big Sky'. Having a jubilant sound, it was a solid choice as a B-side to the 'New World' single. The lyrics subvert the usual Monday morning moaning imagery, bringing an originality to the trope, and evinces how Santa Maria's compositions brought something different to the band. Perhaps splitting his tracks up more would have meant they had a bolder impact.

Whilst Monday is etymologically related to the moon, some listings incorrectly label this song as 'Monday Morning Dance'.

Santa Maria released two solo albums, although the second was sadly posthumous, as he died aged only 37 in 1996.

'Blue' (Sebastian Santa Maria)

From a Genesis-style track to one that recalls Peter Gabriel's solo work, this builds into a potent chorus, swelled by rich keyboards. The thoughtful lyric tells how colour is more articulate than anything else:

Every plain draws its own shade
And every shadow its particular note
That tells you more than anything I ever wrote.

This concept was inspired by the 20th-century French composer Oliver Messiaen, who'd coincidentally taught Pierre Boulez, an influence for 'Butcher's Song'. Messiaen had synaesthesia and heard music in colour, giving each chord its own shade. Santa Maria develops this theme in the lyrics, as Jimi Hendrix had done, particularly on *Axis: Bold As Love*, and uses it in the music, too, as the short but twisty guitar solo evokes a midnight blue in its tones.

'Nights On Fire' (Sebastian Santa Maria)

A celebration of the human spirit, this is a gentle ballad built mostly around an understated acoustic guitar that uses flavours of oriental notes, before relenting to a classically influenced piano line. Shorter than most other tracks, it's a welcome change in tone after the more muscular pieces, with the breathy backing vocals enhancing the fragility.

'Losing You' (Colin Blunstone, Phil Dennys)

Co-written with Phil Dennys, who'd also helped to write 'How Could We Dare To Be Wrong' from Blunstone's *Ennismore*, this is a respectable ballad, but is a little lost on the album, as its minor key and tempo are too similar to what's already passed. A hint of country guitar aims at variation, but it isn't enough to make it stand out. The twists and turns of the melodically intriguing verse work well, and the bursting chorus should have cemented this as a hit. The lyrics hold an effective pun too: 'Another lonely night turns into day/And suddenly the truth has dawned on me'.

'Alone In Paradise' (Andy Nye, Colin Blunstone)

Suffering in much the same way as the previous track by being too like the others, the lyrics here are a little confused and cover some recurrent Blunstone imagery that, by now, is becoming a little worn, e.g. reaching out in darkness, etc. The line 'And paradise is heaven with you' is quite a muddled image. Furthermore, the tone of the keyboards in the opening is dated, and the harmonica solo doesn't emphasise the poignancy as it's supposed to do.

'Knowing You' (Colin Blunstone)

With a simple guitar backing and a delicate melody that recalls the finest parts of *One Year*, and is a quietly stunning track. The overlapping verse and bridge, with Blunstone momentarily duetting with himself, is tinglingly good. If the album had closed here, it would have resolved on an achingly lovely note.

'Love Conquers All' (Colin Blunstone)

Opening with a fanfare of organ, this breezy track boasts an effectively driving bass line, and the guitar runs after the chorus mimic a dramatic ellipsis. It's also a shorter track, so doesn't lose its dynamism with a chorus or two too many, which does plague some of the other tracks. Blunstone experiments with a more conversational tone in the verses and this works surprisingly well. It would probably have been better to split up some of the similar tracks earlier on. However, the spurts of organ on the fade-out recall The Zombies' former sound, showing that it could be tastefully updated.

Conclusion

Grundy told *Goldmine*: 'I'm very proud of *New World*. It's just a shame that it never really quite got the release and the backing that I think it deserved'. It certainly merits a larger audience, but it's a moot point if it can really be called a Zombies album without the indispensable Argent.

Yet, the album is pleasing in itself and includes at least two Zombies tracks that compare seriously with their best in 'Lula Lula' and 'Knowing You', a happier result which would eventually lead to a more authentic Zombies sound re-emerging. This was to follow in 1991 when Colin Blunstone re-recorded 'Time Of The Season', 'She's Not There' and 'Tell Her No' for *Colin Blunstone Sings His Greatest Hits*. This time, Argent took a key role, but Atkinson was unable to contribute. Characteristically, the band then went to ground for a time, perhaps missing out wisely or unwisely on the 1960s revival sparked by Brit Pop. A tribute album appeared in 1994 – *World Of The Zombies* – and featured American power pop bands like Posies and Flop, but also punk acts such as Fastbacks. It drew little attention and seemed to confirm that the band had left a stronger legacy in the US than elsewhere. However, by the end of the 1990s, yet another resurrection was to occur.

Zombie Heaven

But for the miracle, I mean our preservation few in millions
Can speak like us
Gonzalo, William Shakespeare, *The Tempest*

A stylishly presented four-disc set released on 18 November 1997, this is truly essential. Whilst Ian McDonald felt there wasn't enough substantial material to warrant a collection of this size, nearly everyone else disagreed and this excellent set was the catalyst for a reappraisal of the band's significance. Tom Petty contributed insightfully to the liner notes: 'Their music was ethereal, with a groove from somewhere else, with a voice of rough velvet. There was jazz, R&B, even country at times'. Alec Palao writes very detailed notes on the tracks and includes comments by the band, too.

The box set contains *Begin Here*, all the singles, a sizable number of live recordings and demos, the entirety of *Odessey And Oracle* and most of *R.I.P.* (an album featuring tracks recorded by The Zombies between 1964 and 1968 but not released until 2000. It is discussed later in the book). Some might have expected that there would be many undiscovered riches from the *Odessey* sessions, but as these were so tightly rehearsed in a village hall prior to recording, there's not much, but there are alternate versions of 'This Will Be Our Year', 'A Rose For Emily' and a radio advert for 'Time Of The Season'.

However, even without the obvious riches of *Odessey and Oracle*, it's a superb collection that proves the band had much more to offer. My only gripe is having to re-program the CD to hear *Begin Here* properly, as the collection orders these tracks without 'She's Not There'. Their debut single opens the box set, but perhaps it could have been duplicated in its original position, as most fans would be happy to hear it as both a debut single and as an album track.

Here, I take a look at tracks not collected elsewhere.

'I'm Going Home' (Bob Bain)
This is a serviceable rocker, which is sometimes known as 'I'm Going Home (To See My Woman)', but probably the most interesting fact about it is how this was mixed up with 'She's Coming Home' and accidentally released on *The Singles A and B Sides* collection in 1988.

The group were familiar with this track through Gene Vincent's version, although it was written by guitarist Bob Bain. Bain was known for his collaborations with Henry Mancini, including his performing on the soundtracks for *Breakfast at Tiffany's* (he's playing the 'Moonriver' chords that Audrey Hepburn mimes to), the TV series *Peter Gunn* and the Elvis Presley Western *Charro*.

Vincent's version begins with the slow, drawled intro that The Zombies emulate, but also has some jumping saxophone that prevents it from becoming monotonous and lends it a jazz flavour. The Zombies miss the chance to develop this and produce a straightforward RnB cut, but as usual, it's elevated by a brilliantly scribbly organ solo and closes with a climbing riff that is a more original touch than Vincent's fade-out. This song was also performed by The Zombies in their victorious Herts Beat final set.

'Come On Time' (Colin Blunstone/Harold Bunbrin)
This is a re-recording of 'Just Out of Reach' that was used to advertise the film *Bunny Lake Is Missing*.

'One Day I'll Say Goodbye' (Chris White)
This was demoed at Chris's dad's house in 1966 and would later become 'Maybe After He's Gone'. It's remarkable for the deep tone that Blunstone employs, as this isn't heard anywhere else in his work with the band.

'I Don't Want To Worry' (Chris White)
Demoed at the same time as the previous track, this is a mid-tempo song with a passably catchy chorus, but has little else to have made it worth revisiting. The lyrics that recount someone doing everything for the singer are also too similar to terrain already covered.

'A Love That Never Was' (Rod Argent)
This is a pretty little song demoed in October 1966 that should have been recorded properly. However, its debt to The Beatles is obvious, with the middle eight shadowing 'I'll Follow The Sun' with a shiver of Harrison's 'I Want To Tell You', and there's the slipping rhythm of 'That Means A Lot' throughout – albeit, The Zombies had played around with this type of rhythm before. The sweet lead vocal by Argent is appealing and the lyrics reconsider a Zombie obsession through a faint psychedelic tint: 'Living in a dream, vague hallucination, thinking of a love that never was'.

'Call Of The Night' (Chris White)
This would later be recorded as 'Girl Help Me' and appeared on *R.I.P.* The aching melody and the lines of classical piano are effective, as is the haunting lyrical imagery: 'I'll fade as the sun fades from the sky'. This is also of note as Blunstone takes the lead vocal, unlike the one on the *R.I.P.* album.

'Out Of The Day' (Chris White)
This is a mid-tempo number, notable for its sudden shift to a chasing riff that's reminiscent of Neal Hefti's *Batman* theme, or as Argent remarks in the liner notes, 'like Pearl and Dean'. Arriving with a slightly Arabic-sounding guitar riff, it's driven by a pulsing bass line and a looser drum beat. The lyrics are once again decorated with some cautious psychedelic imagery, for example, the 'sunset coloured air'. It's an intriguing track that should have been released at the time.

'Early One Morning' (Richard Penniman)

The gulping bassline is the best thing about this Little Richard cover. Perhaps the gripe about Zombie covers being disposable is not so much about their performance, but rather, their choices…

'For You My Love' (Paul Gayten)

This was written by the pianist Paul Gayten and recorded by Larry Darnell – who scored a US R&B number one with it – where the arrangement was brass-heavy. It had recently been revived by James Brown's album *Showtime* from 1964, which blended horns with a fleet-footed organ line. Argent's piano work on their version is jazzy and light, supported by tightly controlled drumming. It's not the most convincing Blunstone vocal, however.

'Soulville' (Titus Turner, Morris Levy, Henry Glover, Dinah Washington)

Similar to 'Sticks And Stones' in its arrangement and delivery (not surprisingly, both are penned by Titus Turner), this is a typical cover from the early Zombies. It opens with a mournfully slow and pining repetition of the town's name before the RnB backing kicks in. The piano is quite low in the mix, which is a shame, but the guitar and drums are tight together. Being a repetitive track, even though it just crosses the two-minute mark, it drags. Dinah Washington's original cut from 1963 is elevated by some call-and-response backing vocals, and brass that adds flesh to the bones and makes for a more complex listen. Where a sparser backing had made some other Zombies tracks stand out, here it lessens the song.

'Rip It Up' (Robert Blackwell)

Argent told *Goldmine* that he had absolutely no recollection of performing this! Perhaps it was performed more as a filler, but it does have much to recommend it. A hiss of hi-hat and then a jazzy piano line opens this track before Blunstone croons the first verse, and it bursts into the rock 'n' roll standard we're familiar with. It's an interesting variation, but, alas, the mannered backing vocals don't do it any favours. This was recorded for *Top Gear* in February 1965, along with a sterling version of 'Can't Nobody Love You'.

'You Must Believe Me' (Curtis Mayfield)

This is a breezy version of a Curtis Mayfield track, enhanced by a mature vocal from Blunstone and the determined piano bleating in denial: 'it just didn't happen that way'! Tight backing vocals complete the groove and the sparing riffs from Atkinson are winningly understated. The tension between the buoyancy of the delivery and the lyrics, in which the protagonist is desperately trying to get a lover to believe in him, works really well, as in: 'You say be serious, no time for fun'. The Impressions' original is lower, more sober and was the closing track on the classic album *People Get Ready* from 1965. However, The Zombies' twist is effective, heightening the conflict between the couple in this way.

'It's All Right' (Curtis Mayfield)

Another Mayfield cover, this isn't quite as successful as the previous one. Indeed, The Zombies seem to struggle with tracks that are both musically and lyrically upbeat during this period. Whilst *Odessey and Oracle* halts this, they're more convincing in the early days when dealing with the lovelorn or despairing. The Impressions scored their biggest hit with this track, however, and it's not surprising, as theirs is assured and committed.

'Will You Love Me Tomorrow' (Gerry Goffin/Carole King)

The tentative longing in the lyrics, coupled with the pining melody, should make this an ideal song for the talents of The Zombies, and Blunstone in particular. Regrettably, they make it more of a beat song, with the tone set by the opening riff that launches a powerful gallop at odds with the lyric's insecurity. First recorded by The Shirelles in 1960, it was radical in both its treatment of burgeoning sexuality and for being the first US number one by a black female group. Alas, The Zombies strip the track of any radicalism.

Blunstone's vocal is also mannered, with a curious American twang. In some ways, it sounds a bit like Del Shannon and isn't entirely unsuccessful, but leaves the listener wondering if a little more thought, a hint of the uncertainty present on 'She's Not There', might have made this into one of their best covers.

'When The Love Light Starts Shining Through Her Eyes' (Eddie Holland, Lamont Dozier, Brain Holland)

Again, this jaunty song suffers from not being quite as jaunty as it needs to be, and Blunstone isn't singing in his own lovely, pure delivery either, adopting a grating American tone. However, the piano is pleasing and the rhythm changes are handled deftly. This was recorded by The Supremes but is a bit of a throwaway in either guise. To be fair, like many bands of the time, as attested to on The Beatles' *Live At The BBC*, it was a requirement that bands play other contemporary hits, and radio appearances, in particular, were about giving a feeling of the live experience of a club or gig – so, by the standard of the day, this is fine. Yet, when bands housed their own excellent songwriters, these sessions now seem something of a lost opportunity.

'Just A Little Bit' (Rosco Gordon)

Recorded for The Beat Show in 1965, this is powered by a determined riff and has a great portentous Argent solo in the middle that looks ahead to prog. It is undoubtedly one of their best live covers – shame about the poor sound quality, but it is a track well worth discovering. Rosco Gordan penned this in 1959 and recorded it with brass bleating out the distinctive riff that's rumoured to have inspired The Beatles' 'Birthday'. This cover is another example of Argent taking a classic RnB track and re-characterising it with compelling keyboard work, evincing how the non-originals still have something to offer.

'Sitting In The Park' (Billy Stewart)

Marred by poor sound quality, the track is quite sweetly done, but Blunstone struggles with the scansion of that least musical of words 'nevertheless...'. The arrangement is closer to George Fame's dreamier and balmier take, rather than Billy Stewart's more rueful and slower original. Coincidentally, Stewart joined *The Caravan Of Stars* after The Zombies had moved on and he would also record 'Summertime' in 1966, resulting in a dramatic version embellished with scat and some tense brass, with just a shiver of one Neil MacArthur...

'This Old Heart Of Mine' (Eddie Holland, Lamont Dozier)

On safer ground with a bouncy arrangement but lovelorn lyrics, this is one of The Zombies' more successful covers. The Isley Brothers had recently scored a UK and US hit with the song but included the parenthetical '(Is Weak For You)' after the main title.

'The Look Of Love' (Burt Bacharach, Hal David)

Starting more like a piece by Bach than Bacharach, this is a sultry version that allows Blunstone another opportunity to transform into a male Dusty Springfield. The bossa nova rhythm recalls 'She's Not There', of course, but after the mildly radical opening, it's a straightforward reworking.

'Kenny Everett Jingle' (Rod Argent/Chris White)

Everett was one of the earliest supporters of *Odessey And Oracle*, having been a dedicated fan since the band's first hit. He seems genuinely dismayed to hear in the interview how The Zombies are splitting up, even before the release of *Odyssey And Oracle*, which he describes, perhaps only half-archly, as 'the album of the century'.

Conclusion

At the launch of this collection, Blunstone played a solo set singing his own cuts as well as 'A Rose For Emily', 'Tell Her No', 'This Will Be Our Year' and the lesser-spotted 'Indication'. This was followed by an unrehearsed 'She's Not There' and 'Time Of The Season' performed by the whole band. The audience were thrilled. The Zombies were live.

It seems that the band could have exploited this renewed admiration a little more, as the 1990s love affair with the 1960s was in full bloom. Advantageously, the organ sound had been less explored than the power pop side of things, so they could have utilised this more. But as was often the case with the band, their timing was just off, and when The Zombies would record together again, trends had moved on.

In the notes to *Zombie Heaven*, Alec Palao writes, 'In the UK, where it's fair to say they are barely regarded as anything more than an above-average beat group' when referring to the band's lack of local success. The box set marked a shift in attitudes towards the band, but these notes don't mention that *Odessy And Oracle* had already ranked 97 in *Mojo*'s 100 Greatest Albums of All Time in 1995. Therefore, they had not been entirely overlooked in the interim, but it did certainly prove the impetus for yet another resurrection...

R.I.P. (The Lost Album)

Personnel
Colin Blunstone: lead vocals,
Rod Argent: keyboards
Chris White: bass, vocals
Paul Atkinson: guitar
Hugh Grundy: drums
Jim Rodford: bass
Rick Birkett: guitar
Recorded: Decca Studios, Trident Studios, Landsdowne Studios, Morgan Studios
Producer: Rod Argent/Chris White
Engineer: Gus Dudgeon
Release Date: 25 October 2000
Chart placings: UK: did not chart

Our revels now are ended
Prospero, William Shakespeare, *The Tempest*

This most posthumous of releases, *R.I.P.* marked both the end of The
Zombies in the 1960s and signalled the new direction that Argent would take.
Taking a cheeky pun as its title, it had an almost plain black cover as though
in mourning. Also known as *The Lost Album*, despite plans for this collection
to be a bridge between the extinct band and their next incarnation, it was
shelved, finding daylight in 2000, although, of course, *Zombie Heaven* had
harboured some of these tracks. Yet, it makes sense to examine it as a distinct
Zombies album, as this was the original intention.

Engineer Gus Dudgeon had been so admiring of the band as both
musicians and people that he agreed to come back for a much-reduced fee
to help record it; Dudgeon, Argent and White's recording skills make for a
consistently punchy but clean sound.

The first half, broadly speaking, is the more reflective and is recorded post-
Zombies proper, whilst the second part, beginning with 'If It Don't Work Out',
looks as far back as 1964, but also rounds up some later cuts with Blunstone
on vocals. In some ways, the album moves from experience to innocence, in
opposition to *Odessey And Oracle*.

'She Loves The Way They Love Her' (Rod Argent, Chris White)
Having heard both Blunstone's smooth performance and the demo version
from *Into the Afterlife*, before this recording, it was something of an anti-
climax: the audience sounds and the intro piece evokes a variety show, and
it means that this recording hovers dangerously close to the novelty song.
Whilst making for an effective opener in general, perhaps with *Sgt. Pepper* in
mind, it just errs too much on the frivolous. Sadly, lacking is the wry piano
from the demo that meant this bubble-gum pop kept a keen edge.

Like 'Smokey Day', 'I Know She Will',' If It Don't Work Out', 'Conversation Off Floral Street', 'Don't Cry For Me' and 'Walking In The Sun', this was first released on *Time Of The Zombies* in 1973.

'Imagine The Swan' (Rod Argent, Chris White)
This was released as a single in 1969 and further details can be found in that chapter. Sadly, the track drags more as part of an album, especially sandwiched between two such strong tracks. It emphasises an unfortunate similarity to the tremulous solo work of Robin Gibb.

'Smokey Day' (Rod Argent, Chris White)
Blunstone said this was his favourite track when he covered it on *One Year,* and the crepuscular atmosphere is tenderly evoked, with coppery guitar and shivers of woodwind. Although Blunstone would also sing this gloriously, the harmonies here are at once ephemeral and powerful like an autumn wind. Not only supremely lovely in terms of the music, but it's also one of the strongest and most sensual lyrics, recounting the clarity of day relenting to the evening, and, with it, half-reminisces, all of which could be quoted here. However, the highlights include: 'soft serene she dances' and 'dulcet vesper voices', using sibilance to hint at a slinking mist, something half-seen. The fall in the phrase 'Smokey Day' insinuates inertia and the singer fighting for breath ever so slightly in the gloom. The shift from the suspended to the minor in the melody line as it reaches 'Voices calling gently for the night' is a skin-tingling moment, as is the unexpectedly jazzy piano solo. In some ways, this track blends the madrigal feel of 'Changes' with the cool, jazzier 'She's Not There' Zombies sound – a seductive melange.

'Girl, Help Me' (Rod Argent, Chris White)
This is one of those moody songs that White performed effectively with a brooding backing. The lyrics are incisive too, with some striking images of isolation and disappointment: 'Last night I walked out to a darkening sky/I heard a sad song, and the song made me cry' and 'For when I was young with the fever of life/Your love cut my soul like a blade of a knife'. The darkening imagery also provides an affecting link to the previous track, and the suspended chords keep the song in mid-air with the singer left to struggle. The slight ascent then drops to a minor on the chorus and this also emphasises how the singer is trapped, supported by a deceptively simple melody that coheres well with the lyric. The echo on the vocal in the middle eight ranks up the pathos and looks back to one of Ken Jones's techniques.

'I Could Spend The Day' (Rod Argent, Chris White)
This pensive track, sung by Argent, is said to have been inspired by Beethoven and it's a dreamy ballad that suffers from being positioned too close to songs of the same temperament on this collection. However, the

piano glissandos are a standout and shine as they follow an angelic harmony line that would have displayed Blunstone's voice beautifully.

'Conversation Off Floral Street' (Rod Argent, Chris White)
This is a cleverly placed track on the album as it helps it to shift from the pensive to the optimistic; it also separates the songs with Argent on lead from those with Blunstone's vocals. Nevertheless, the sequencing might have worked better if this had been more mixed, especially as so many of the songs in the second half have a similar atmosphere.
See also *Zombie Heaven*.

'If It Don't Work Out' (Rod Argent)
Blunstone uses the thinner tone that he sometimes adopts on the rockier numbers, saving a richer register for the middle eight. This helps to break up the poppier numbers, lending some much-needed variation. The yelping strings on the chorus evoke just a hint of mania, counteracting the buoyancy and optimism of this side of the album.
See 'Singles 1969'.

'I'll Call You Mine' (Chris White)
A ridiculously strong pop song, this should have been hummed by milkmen up and down the country. The ebullient melody is captured perfectly in the piano arrangement and has one of Blunstone's most committed vocals. The Chopin-esque solo is a joy to behold.

'I'll Keep Trying' (Rod Argent)
If The Zombies could afford to leave this excellent song in the vaults, then it's an immense testament to the abundance of riches they had to offer. In fact, as this song follows more of a traditional structure (verse, bridge, chorus, etc.) than some tracks chosen for single release, this might have been a wiser choice. A particular highlight is how the guitar and keyboard tones blend seamlessly to keep a deliciously nagging riff going.

Not only are Argent and White's superior songwriting skills on display, but also their production abilities. All of the tracks are mixed very well, particularly 'I'll Keep Trying', which, under Ken Jones, might have suffered from a submerged vocal potentially drowned by the racing guitar and bass; yet, this and the rumbling drums are layered exceptionally well. This is a pleasing slice of power pop that, when combined with 'I'll Call You Mine', creates one of the most unapologetically exultant sections of a pop album.

'I Know She Will' (Chris White)
Appearing first on the compilation *Time of the Zombies* from 1974, this includes a wistful string arrangement by Mike Vickers of Manfred Mann. It also evinces Argent and White's mastery of dynamics, as the track rises and

falls in a way that could overwhelm or become tiresome but is compellingly executed here.

'Don't Cry For Me' (Chris White)
Too many songs with common themes or atmospheres are bunched together, which weakens the album. On the one hand, we might refer to them as movements in a longer piece, but it can also mean that strong songs drift by without receiving the attention they deserve. Yet, it's worth listening carefully because the backing vocals alone make this a great addition to the album and show that stereo mixes can offer something new.

'Walking In The Sun' (Rod Argent)
A fitting finale for an album of unabashed optimism, growing from the dusky opening tracks to the ebullience of a new morning heralded by gloriously resonant drums. The rhythmic intro riff has shades of The Spencer Davies Group's 'Gimme Me Some Loving', even though it's unlikely they'd heard this track, as it wasn't officially released at the time. The band recorded it in 1965, but Mike Vickers overdubbed the orchestral arrangement in 1969.

It's full of hooks, from the assured opening to the hint of echo on the verse vocals; from the glamourous sweeping strings of the verse compared to their staccato delivery leading into the bridge, to the burst of the pre-chorus and the descent for the chorus proper. In fact, The Zombies' songs often have two choruses as opposed to a bridge and a chorus, such is their power. And it makes it all the more mystifying why hits were consistently elusive. The diminished chords, used carefully, create a slight tension, illuminating the contrast between the singer's blessed position and his observation about others: 'If they only knew....'. However, the bridge, in which this line appears, has the bass almost jumping for joy, sustaining the sunshine throughout. A glorious track that, in some ways, would be the template for Blunstone's early career – with strings being used for both romantic and rockier effect.

Bonus Tracks
'I'm Goin' Home' (Bob Bain)
This marked the first official release of this track after it was mistakenly included on the American collection *Early Days* in place of 'She's Coming Home'.

'Nothing's Changed' (Chris White)
This was included on the *Bunny Lake Is Missing* soundtrack, although not included in the film itself. However, it had been released before this on the May 1965 collection *The Lord's Taverner's Charity Album*, an organisation that supports green spaces, which also boasted The Rolling Stones' 'Surprise Surprise' and The Applejacks' cover of The Beatles' 'Baby's In Black'. More pertinently to The Zombies, however, was Unit 4 + 2's rockabilly track 'Woman From Liberia'. Unit 4 + 2 were also a Hertfordshire band, who'd

officially have their ranks swelled by later Argent members: Russ Ballard joined in 1967, although he plays as a session musician on their number one hit 'Concrete And Clay' from 1965; future Argent drummer Bob Henrit also appeared on this.

A gentle melody with a folk feel, this isn't as memorable as it lacks a strong hook, but it is an agreeable listen and would lead to some stronger songs in a similar vein. It marked a transition from the moodier White compositions to ones with a pronounced romantic feel, and with more optimistic lyrics than the title suggests: they'll be reunited like nothing's changed. For a time, the only Zombies release, this was available on the compilation *The World Of The Zombies* from 1970

Conclusion

This is the least varied of the 'original' Zombies albums as it lilts between brooding, twilit songs and sunshine power pop. Whilst there's a coherence in this, it can mean that the listener really does have to focus if the songs aren't to run into each other, especially in the second half. This isn't helped by the newest songs coming first and the oldest last, although it works as a reverse *Odessey And Oracle*, moving from experience to innocence, in a sense. Nevertheless, it's a fine collection, if still more of a compilation than an album. Although frustrating for this not to have been released at the time, it would likely have diluted the unusual, but absolute loveliness of *Odessey And Oracle* if it had.

A Japanese pressing of this album (*R.I.P. Plus – Zombies Complete Collection Vol. 4*) also includes 'I'm Goin' Home', 'Nothing's Changed', 'Remember You (OST Version)', 'I'll Keep Trying (Undubbed)', 'I Know She Will (Undubbed)', 'Prison Song (Care Of Cell 44) (Backing Track)', 'A Rose For Emily (Alternate Mix 1)', 'A Rose For Emily (Alternate Mix 2)' and 'Time Of The Season (Alternate Mix) as bonus tracks. A later release from 2014 by US label Varese Sarabande adds 'Imagine The Swan (Mono Single Mix)', 'Smokey Day (Mono Mix)', 'If It Don't Work Out (Mono Single Mix)' and 'Don't Cry For Me (Mono Single Mix)'.

Out Of The Shadows – Billed As Colin Blunstone And Rod Argent

Personnel
Colin Blunstone: lead vocals, backing vocals
Rod Argent: piano, Hammond organ, keyboards, backing vocals
Jim Rodford: bass, backing vocals
Dave Bronze: bass on 'Helpless', 'Danger Zone', fretless bass on 'Love Can Heal The Pain'
Mark Johns: guitar
Clem Clemson: guitar on 'Helpless', 'Sanctuary' and 'Danger Zone'
Steve Rodford: drums, percussion
Peter Van Hooke: drums, percussion on 'Helpless', 'Sanctuary' and 'Mystified', percussion on 'Danger Zone'
Steve Sidwell: trumpet
Phil Todd: saxophone
Recorded: Redhouse Studios
Producer: Mathew White
Engineer: Nick Robbins
UK Release Date: 2001
Chart placings: UK: did not chart

So I charmed their ears ...
Ariel, William Shakespeare, *The Tempest*

Sharing a title with a Shadows album from 1962, this album isn't credited to The Zombies officially but is the beginning of their final resurrection. Admittedly, there's a good argument that this is a Rod Argent solo album with Blunstone stepping in for the vocals, as the backing musicians include many who'd played on Argent's 1988 collection *Red House*, such as guitarist Clem Clempson, bassist Dave Bronze, saxophonist Phil Todd and drummer Peter Van Hooke, but it's an important step in the band's reformation.

For the first time on a recording, Argent and Blunstone are joined by Jim Rodford's son Steve on drums. Argent told Tom Golloway: 'Steve is incredibly musical. What I love about him is he's technically very good, but he listens. He listens to what you're playing and he responds to it and I love that'.

Colin Blunstone said of the album to *It's Psychedelic, Baby* magazine:

I had six concerts coming up and a keyboard player who had a habit of not turning up. On a whim, I decided to ask Rod if he was interested in playing 'live' again and was quite surprised when he said he was, although he emphasised he would only want to do these specific six concerts. In the end, we had such good fun that we just kept going and have now been playing together in this incarnation of the band for over 16 years. Rod already had some basic tracks recorded for a possible new album and we finished these tracks off and added a couple of new songs, and that became our new first album with this incarnation of the band.

'Home' (Rod Argent)

Opening with a piano ballad doesn't make for the most dynamic entrance, and indeed, the song would be more favourably and fairly received if arriving later. The fact that its subject matter – longing for the warmth of home – is not a remarkable one also hinders it. Yet, there are, as we'd expect, some interesting chord changes, particularly in the bridge, but these lead to a bathetic chorus. What is undeniable is the assurance and bronzy gleam of Blunstone's vocal – a constant highlight of the album.

'A Girl Like That' (Rod Argent/Russ Ballard)

Co-written by Argent's old bandmate Russ Ballard, this is one of the most memorable tracks and is evidence of how The Zombies' sound could be updated judiciously: it would undoubtedly have made a strong album opener. It's a guitar-driven piece whose circular lyrics are an anti-'She's Not There', recounting instead a reliable presence. Mark John's solo begins in a brooding mood before squalling out and giving way to a superlative Hammond organ solo by Argent that's as warm as Blunstone's voice.

'Helpless' (Rod Argent)

Covering some similar ground lyrically as the verses of 'I Want You Back Again', this does throw up some variations on the theme: 'I want to communicate/Try so hard, but my tongue frustrates'. Sadly, the arrangement is redolent of Toto and sounds more old-fashioned than anything from *Begin Here*! The melody has a gospel feel that would have been worth exploring a little more in the backing, but Clem Clempson's smooth guitar tone is a highlight.

The band are plagued once more by being out of their time: if this had been released in the 1980s, it would have seemed a solid and serviceable collection. To be fair, many artists had to get this sound of their system, but it's frustrating that Argent and Blunstone didn't take advantage of Britpop or the 1990s veneration of the 1960s to relaunch an authentic, if modified sound.

'Sanctuary' (Rod Argent)

A balmy song with a few degrees of 'Summertime' in its melody, this is a breezy track powered by rhythm guitar and given speed by a fleet-footed bassline. The cooing keyboard is just right, too. Romantic lyrics take an unexpected turn of phrase: 'Sympathy, warmth and understanding/With every breath of your love bequeathed'. There's something of the sultry atmosphere of 'Andorra' here but with a warm narrative instead of a rancorous one.

'Living In The Real World' (Rod Argent)

A soft rock track in the style of Boston, it's evident that they were chasing an American sound for this album. Understandable, given that they achieved success there, but their unique tones seem compromised. Tracks like this see them pursuing styles that don't suit Argent's musicianship, and whilst Blunstone's vocals are always polished, they can't lift a predictable melody.

'Mystified' (Rod Argent)

This track makes the album's problems all the more apparent – multiple songs are mid-tempo and meander on for too long. This is an agreeable boogie, but when one considers that The Zombies' defining and more complicated tracks barely got to three minutes, a sense of discipline is evidently lacking. It's undoubtedly catchy and The Zombies (as they would soon return to this name) would add it to their later live set, where it makes for a bouncier listen.

'Only The Rain' (Rod Argent/Mark Argent)

A curious and oddly beautiful song, this was partly written by Argent's son Mark. The lyrics and music are the most well-matched on the album with some striking imagery, as in 'And the rain fell, like ball bearings on a roulette wheel/Eliminating the future' and the Chris White-esque 'The stars arranged themselves like an illuminated skipping rope'. The melody mimics the motif of rain with an almost free-form feel at times. The piano solo is understated with a jazz flavour before it returns for the closing and ripples gorgeously. Mark John's guitar adds warmth to a beautifully romantic piece.

'Baby Don't You Cry No More' (Rod Argent)

ABBA's Frida Lyngstad recorded a rather twee version for her album *Something's Going On* in 1982. Argent and Blunstone give it a jolt of power, but the melody is a generic lounge bar lilt. The cadences of the organ solo compensate, as do the lambent guitar licks, but the track merely drifts by.

'Danger Zone' (Rod Argent)

After a weary, sparsely backed opening sung by Blunstone, lamenting that he can't give a reason to his lover for his impending dread, the track veers into a Motown-inspired, lively pop track, complete with Supremes-style backing vocals from Argent. It also contains horns, a rarity for The Zombies, with Steve Sidwell's trumpet and Phil Todd's saxophone swelling the sound. Clempson's storming guitar solo and Dave Bronze's rumbling bass stop things from being too frothy, and the band seem to be enjoying themselves enormously. This would have made for a catchy single.

'Love Can Heal The Pain' (Rod Argent)

Opening quietly, with gentle guitar and piano, the melody takes an interesting turn with some unexpected chords in the chorus. The image of rain recurs, representing how love can cleanse; it's a softly optimistic closing to the album. Like the previous track, this seems to owe something to 1960s soul with wisps of Smokey Robinson and is smoothly sung by Blunstone.

Conclusion

Mostly ignored by the music press on release, the album is certainly worth a listen, but it has to be said that, whilst the songs by themselves are not necessarily weak, together, they lack impact, or perhaps there isn't enough of an identifiable sound, despite some outstanding musicianship. However, 'Sanctuary' and 'A Girl Like You' in particular, promised that this collaboration could go further.

As Far As I Can See

Personnel
Colin Blunstone: lead vocals,
Rod Argent: keyboards, backing vocals, lead vocals with Blunstone on 'South Side Of The Street'
Jim Rodford: bass, backing vocals
Keith Airey: lead guitar
Steve Rodford: drums
Mark Johns: rhythm guitar
Chris White: backing vocals
Andrew Powell: conductor
Producer: Rod Argent
Engineer: Steve Orchard
UK Release: 5 May 2004
Chart placings: UK: did not chart

> Awake, dear heart, awake. Thou hast slept well. Awake.
> **Prospero, William Shakespeare, *The Tempest***

Unfairly savaged by critics for what was perceived as MOR music and vapid lyrics, this is perhaps the least loved album in the band's collection, but it's a return to The Zombies' glory days in many ways. Even when Argent and Blunstone were assiduous about not being The Zombies, they found themselves billed as such at so many gigs that they realised there was definitely a hunger for the band and it didn't really make sense to deny this. Blunstone told Aaron Badgely for *Pitchfork* in 2023:

> When we got back together, we toured as Colin Blunstone and Rod Argent, we didn't call ourselves The Zombies. We hardly play any Zombie's tunes. We each had our solo careers. Then we just realised people were asking for Zombie songs. We got together with the other surviving members and said, 'look, we are playing Zombie concerts, do you mind if we use the name The Zombies?' It seemed more honest to do that, and they agreed and we started touring as The Zombies.

The album also has two other Zombies involved, if only scantly. Paul Atkinson used his A&R skills to promote the work but sadly passed away before its release, aged only 58. Chris White is on backing vocals; however, this rather tentative appearance might give a clue about his feelings on the project ...
Robert Christgau's review was lacerating: '...the music is craven crap ... chlock orchestrations, socko choruses, showtime overstatements bound for the casino circuit'. He also took exception with the imagery of escape and moving on, especially as the direction they were headed in couldn't seriously compare with their other work, both in and out of The Zombies. However, a

closer listen shows that, whilst not completely inaccurate, it's mostly wide of the mark. Striking strings conducted by Andrew Powell (of The Alan Parsons Project and Kate Bush fame especially), fragile melodies and Blunstone's gleaming tones abound.

'In My Mind A Miracle' (Rod Argent)

This opener recounts the transformative power of love, likening finding a lover to discovering an 'odessey and oracle'. Some critics called opportunism on this reference ... No matter, the track does update The Zombies' sound well overall.

Beginning with a 'Time Of The Season' beat and then a rising bleating riff, backed with strings and a wash of organ, this has shivers of funk, and is better than the reviews would have us believe. Blunstone and Argent's harmonies on the chorus are ardent and the keyboard solo ripples joyously. Perhaps a fade out at this point would have kept the impact of the track, as another verse and chorus weigh it down.

The track was released as a single backed with a longer live version.

'Memphis' (Rod Argent)

A stately string arrangement announces this ballad before a swirl of piano notes join and Blunstone's gentle vocals describe 'shimmering waves of moonlight' and 'the breath of angels'. Using imagery of both Egypt and Presley's Memphis, this mini-epic celebrates the longevity of love and its ability to liberate; it also re-uses the motif of flight and perspective with its gliding chorus: 'tonight my soul has wings'. The arrangement dips and lifts like flight itself and mirrors 'seeing with an eagle's eye'. The idea of a bird's eye view, or music that implies a towering perspective, is to be found across the album as a whole.

'South Side Of The Street' (Rod Argent)

A happy-go-lucky boogie, Argent and Blunstone take turns at the bouncy verses before duetting on the last one. The lyrics seem to draw inspiration from the classic 'On The Sunny Side Of The Street', a track with music by Jimmy McHugh and lyrics by Dorothy Fields, and recount moving into happier times. The idea of different perspectives is called upon again here: 'I tried my best, but I could not cope/From the end of a telescope'. Perhaps it's too much of a stretch to make a link back to 'Mr. Galileo...'

The middle eight has an irresistible spring and the backing vocals glister beautifully behind Blunstone like little twinkles of sunlight. Unsurprisingly, this irresistibly optimistic pop song was released as a single with 'As Far As I Can See' as the B-Side.

'I Want To Fly' (Rod Argent)

This excellent song is reminiscent of the mood of *One Year*, with Blunstone's melancholy vocals and a gorgeous string arrangement melding magically together. It's a song of longing for freedom that closes with a clever unresolved chord as Blunstone grieves: 'Bathed in starlight/Birds wheel hard across the sky' whilst he cannot 'leave the ordinary world'. The album shifts between flights of fancy and freedom and laments for being grounded in the wrong place, and this is most successfully realised here. In some ways, the lyrics develop Argent's 'Be Free' from their debut album, but here, the singer is yearning for this escape, whilst previously, it was advice to another, a little like in the tradition of 'She's Not There' before the band then moved on to writing more directly about the speaker's feelings.

Argent's string arrangement is both romantic and tense. The middle eight has a dramatic surge and some Jeff Lynne-style backing vocals, with a shiver too of the coda of ELO's 'Shangri La'. This track alone should have proved to critics that The Zombies' afterlife had much more to give. It's no wonder, then, that the band revisited it for *Different Game* in 2023.

'Time To Move' (Rod Argent)

A rocker in the vein of their older RnB covers, with a shade of 'I Saw Her Standing There' in the melody, this track changes the atmosphere after the reflective 'I Want to Fly'. It's a tight performance by the band, giving everyone a chance to stand out, but especially Keith Airey with a blistering guitar solo. The other tracks are defined more by the strings and it might be that The Zombies' identity as a band (albeit a new and emerging version), rather than as Blunstone and Argent, is diluted by this, but this track foreshadows how the players would come together better on later albums and particularly live performances.

'I Don't Believe In Miracles' (Russ Ballard)

This is, of course, a re-recording of Russ Ballard's aching ballad, and it's no coincidence that it's also the album's shortest track, being a beautifully constructed song. It uses a broad and complex range of chords to keep the melody as uncertain as the jilted singer is. There's a familiar Zombies trope in the use of a suspended chord, which reflects a lyrical uncertainty: 'I believe I was your game, your ball/If you tossed me up then I would fall'.

Ballard told Henry Yates at *Classic Rock* in 2020 about the son's genesis:

My parents had both been really ill; my dad had prostate cancer and my mum had bowel cancer at the same time. I'd felt so low. During that period, I remember writing 'I Don't Believe In Miracles', and at the end of the song, I just put my head down on the piano keys and cried.

The track opened Blunstone's second album *Ennismore* and also featured Argent and Rodford. It was released as a single, unjustly lingering outside of the Top 30. Being simultaneously tender and defiant, the original is one of Blunstone's best vocals, perfectly reflecting the dichotomy in the lyric between his lover being a saviour and an adversary: 'The bullet that shot me down came from your gun/The words that turned me round were from your song'.

This version has a similar arrangement, evincing Blunstone's vocal ability had remained just as strong with perhaps even better control of sustain. The piano has a slightly bluesier edge and there are some prominent backing vocals, but the strings seem a little too intense for the subtle melody. However, it's a clever choice to include as it inverts the imagery of the opening track.

'I Don't Believe In Miracles' has been covered by America and Barbara Dickson, whom Jim Rodford backed many times, but neither display the gorgeous vulnerability of Blunstone.

'As Far As I Can See' (Rod Argent)
Blunstone's collaboration with The Alan Parson Project, 'Old and Wise' opens with 'As far as my eyes can see/There are shadows approaching me', and this track takes some of its lyrical inspiration from it, as the song is a cautious acceptance of changing times. A cool string arrangement with shades of Gershwin propels it and slick guitar notes coil around this strikingly. Argent's solo is both relaxed and acute in the 'Summertime' vein and sounds like the 'blue horizon' that reassures the singer. The phrase 'blue horizon' sums up the mood of many tracks on this album, in fact.

'With You Not Here' (Rod Argent)
Ambiently similar to the previous track, this is where the album dips. There's also a clumsy inversion as the title seems to allude to 'She's Not There'. The lyrics were criticised for being trite on this album and generally, this isn't fair. Personally, if the words simply serve apposite and effective melodies, it seems allowable, but here, the imagery is too worn, with rain and grey skies predominating. The rising chords that seem to promise more in the bridge are an elegant touch, but the track doesn't really come alive and would have benefited from some sharp editing.

'Wings Against The Sun' (Rod Argent)
A more successful ballad than the previous one, incorporating an inflection of jazz, it is embellished with some wistful strings that again evoke *One Year*. The wispy harmonies are serene and the melody, although more robust, does have a wisp of 'Misty Roses', which is established in the opening verse: 'In your eyes appear the mystic roses'. The imagery of 'Smoky Day' is elicited, too and the song has a hazy twilight feel. It's a short but quietly powerful track.

'Together' (Rod Argent)
A McCartney-esque song, this is a sweet little thing with some pretty flourishes of classical guitar. The middle eight has a dramatic heave with the minor key shift: 'Have to love you/As much as seasons have to change in

time'. This track looks back, then, melodically and lyrically, and the resolved piano notes at the close imply a satisfaction lacking on 'I Want to Fly'. With this in mind, it probably would have made for a more memorable closing to the album.

'Look For A Better Way' (Rod Argent)

The longest track on the album, it opens with some dated keyboards before a rather hesitant melody develops in the verse. In terms of the criticism of the album being hackneyed or predictable, it's a fairer comment on this track. The rise in the chorus, however, is compensation, with some Harriosn-esque chords in the chorus and at the end of the guitar solo. It allows the album to resolve the idea of perspectives and learning from seeing things as new, as in 'I grab my future from the past mistakes/Some kind of revolution' and 'Each lesson learned is a book/If we can look for a part to play'.

Conclusion

Whilst this is unlikely to be anyone's favourite of the later Zombies albums, it is certainly professional and polished, and Argent began to be able to capture a sense of The Zombies' past. It's also unabashedly romantic with some truly lovely moments, and the loose concept of perspectives marks a sort of ending and a beginning for the band. Whilst some might say that an album about flight and use of the bird's eye view to see things differently is banal, it can be asserted that The Zombies themselves had begun to be seen newly themselves and as much more than also-rans. It also has to be said that this album has more in common with The Zombies of the 1960s than *New World*. Admittedly, I have a fondness for it as I saw them live at this time with my dad, briefly meeting them as they signed my copy, so it has a certain shimmer, regardless. But even Argent himself seemed dismissive of the work. Dave Thompson, writing for *Goldmine* in 2011, commented: 'A new, largely orchestral album, *As Far As I Can See* was released in 2004, but Argent shrugs it off. "It was deliberately done as Colin's voice with strings; it was made to be that"'. By this measure, then, it's a success.

Into The Afterlife (2007)

The clouds methought
Would open and show riches
Ready to drop upon me
Caliban, William Shakespeare, *The Tempest*

Whilst the liner notes of this album make it clear that this isn't actually an official Zombies collection, its title and packaging are less ingenuous, as the band name is used on the front. However, whilst it isn't technically part of their album catalogue, it does include a few of their recordings not collected elsewhere. Perhaps controversially, I'm also exploring it more as an album set rather than as a compilation because it was billed as a sequel to *Zombie Heaven*, which had its own chapter, so I will follow the same logic here. Furthermore, as some of these tracks were being recorded, the band were enjoying a last gasp of success, and whilst it seems that they were adamant they wouldn't reform, it must have at least crossed their minds that some of this work could just possibly end up as part of The Zombies songbook. It also makes for a surprisingly coherent and pleasing listen, opening with a suspenseful 'She's Not There' by the solo Blunstone and ending with a live performance of 'Going To A Go Go' from The Zombies proper; it would be churlish not to take a closer look in detail.

'She's Not There' (Rod Argent)
Credited to Neil MacArthur, aka Colin Blunstone, the shivery vocals leave no doubt as to who this is. It's an arresting alternative being built around a torrid Santana-esque guitar from Big Jim Sullivan. In fact, there are few instruments not thrown at this theatrical reworking, which amused Rod Argent. There are twitchy bass fills between the verse and chorus provided by Led Zeppelin's John Paul Jones, a blusteringly impatient rhythm guitar from producer Mike Hurst, cinematic strings and even some Jethro Tull-style woodwind. It stands up to all of this remarkably well; whilst it obviously doesn't eclipse the original, it's a diverting interpretation nevertheless.

It was released as a single backed with the delicate 'World Of Glass' in 1969 and reached 34 on the UK chart, being Neil MacArthur's most successful song. Also included on this collection, as the last track, is the Italian language version, which lends it a quasi-operatic vibe and makes for an impactful, if ironic, closing.

After The Zombies, Blunstone was feeling jaded by the music business and took a job in insurance, where he worked for almost two years. This was curtailed when Hurst suggested they record a hyperbolic version of the track that had first helped him to secure stardom, in order to relaunch him. Hurst also gave him a pseudonym – a marketing gimmick, but probably also a safe way of easing Blunstone back into the industry. Not that his identity remained a mystery for long! Hurst had first called him James MacArthur, unaware that *Hawaii Five-O*'s Danno was played by an actor with this name. Whilst Blunstone wouldn't feel comfortable in this guise or with the direction these songs were taking for long, 'She's Not There' did become something of a talisman for him as he would record the track at other crossroads in his career.

'Hung Upside Down' (Stephen Stills)

Neil Macarthur might not have managed to surpass the original with the previous track, but succeeds here. The Buffalo Springfield cut certainly has two effective guitar sounds, one thin and precise, the other wavy and thicker, but it lacks Blunstone's mellifluous vocals, which seem to caress the listener. Hung upside down he may be, but he certainly seems to be enjoying it with the suggestive promise of 'What I bring you when I get straight'. The brass building towards the climax swells the passion, but one wonders if a more stripped-back arrangement akin to 'The Way I Feel Inside' would have been just as effective, as the singing alone is thrilling.

'Unhappy Girl' (Rod Argent/Chris White)

Sharing a title and a similar theme with The Doors' cut from 1967's *Strange Days*, this makes evocative use of lachrymose piano with notes dropping like tears. Chris White explained to Palao: 'I wrote 'Unhappy Girl' after The Zombies, and it was a bit of a follow-on from 'Brief Candles'. A young girl of 16, and the loss of innocence. One of those Charles Aznavour-type songs!'

Blunstone would later record this backed by the Argent band but found it a challenging pitch in which to sing.

'She Loves The Way They Love Her' (Rod Argent/Chris White)

A springier version than the (very similar) one which opens Blunstone's exquisite *One Year* from 1971, which was the first track to be recorded for that album. This recounts a wannabe longing to be 'shining in the microphone'. Opening with a bouncy piano riff, it has Argent on vocals, doing his best 'breathy' Blunstone. It also has The Zombies' trademark claps, although this time, they may be more ironic given the topic of the song. Another seemingly optimistic touch with a sharper edge is the playful riff that is really a descending sequence, meaning that the starstruck heroine is walking downstage, lending an ambiguity to the track.

Argent and White played this song to Mickie Most, who ultimately rejected it, feeling it wouldn't be a hit. It should have been.

'Telescope (Mr. Galileo)' (Rod Argent/Chris White)

A curio from White, this is a paean to Galileo's invention (although other names have been cited as the instrument's originator), praising it for helping a voyeur to spy on a girl. It belongs in that peculiarly 1960s category of *faux naïf* songs that recount the actually terrifying peccadilloes of its characters. Looking at the first verse:

I can see her
She can't see me
Oh no, no she can't know
Just where I'll be
See the sun kiss her skin as I sit up in this tree
And we will watch her all day long, my telescope and me

We can see a similarity with The Idle Race's 'Sitting In My Tree' from their debut album, *The Birthday Party*, in the autumn of 1968:

I often sit alone up in a tree
Waving to the ones that wave at me {...}
What they don't know is I am counting them
I even count the ladies and the men.

Even as recently as Paul McCartney's 2007 *Memory Almost Full*, the idea of an outcast hiding up high was returned to on the quirky 'Mr. Bellamy'.

The second version of this track on the album has the title stripped back to 'Mr. Galileo' only. White told Palau of the lascivious vocal: 'This is the dirty version... It was also quite sinister!'

The attack of the riff is reminiscent of the Batman theme (this modish piece, of course, inspired The Who, The Kinks and The Beatles too) and hints at a sense of childishness. The riff echoes The Kinks' 'All day and All of the Night', also implying the implacable determination of the voyeur, further emphasised by the descending scale. One wonders how this would have come off in Blunstone's wispy tones...

'Walking In The Sun' (Rod Argent)
This version had been previously released on *R.I.P.* and returns this collection to a more traditionally romantic focus after the creepy former track.

'Without Her' (Harry Nilsson)
This is definitely in the category of Blunstone as 'Dusty Springfield in drag', with its lounge bar feel. The trumpet is a good touch, developing from the first resigned solo to a mournful bleat on the fade-out. Blunstone recorded the superior vocal live with the band, but it does skirt too close to easy listening for comfort, whereas the Nilsson original, from *The Pandemonium Shadow Show* in 1967, has more of a Baroque feel.

'Twelve Twenty-Nine' (Chris Sedgwick, Peter Lee Stirling)
Whilst a beautifully performed track by Blunstone, the arrangement is too laid back. Written by Chris Sedgwick and Daniel Boone, and previously recorded by Priscilla Paris, it's a familiar tale of a lost love being hurried out of one's life by rail. It would have benefited from a backing more in the style of 'I Remember

When I Loved Her' to prevent it from becoming too whimsical. However, the sad gasp of flute at the end is a wry touch, evoking the train's whistle.

'It Never Fails To Please Me' (Rod Argent/Chris White)
A rambunctious ode to music itself, this has the energy of The Zombies' 'Got My Mojo Working', and boasts a thundering bassline. The switch from rock 'n' roll boogie piano to a classical flourish in the solo is a typically eclectic detail from Argent. The only snag is the grating tone used on the guitar.

'I Could Spend The Day' (Rod Argent/Chris White)
A mellow ballad with Argent taking the lead vocal, this holds back on the keyboards, initially being driven by a sloping guitar riff until the piano trips in before a very effective solo that blends baroque flourishes with a barroom boogie. The lyrics boast some poetic touches: 'Sunlight gently cheers/Too deep, I sweep our eyes', in a lyric that wants to 'laze time away with gentle feeling of life.'

'I Know She Will' (Chris White)
This initially delicate track could have been at home on *Odessey And Oracle*, such is the masterful handling of the rise and fall in the melody and the light and shade in the strings. The surge from fragile to powerful is the song's strongest hook and a trademark of The Zombies.

'Don't Try To Explain' (Billy Vera)
A smooth ballad with a powerful but understated vocal, it's marred by the thinly bleating organ that doesn't leave the verse alone. However, the bass is resonant and expressive.

'World Of Glass' (Mike Hurst)
Producer Mike Hurst, who had been in The Springfield's, wrote this sweet tune that's given a lace-like fragility by a finger-picked guitar. The swirling strings bestow a romantic glamour and it proved a contrast as the B-Side to Neil Macarthur's 'She Not There'.

'To Julia (For When She Smiles)' (Rod Argent/Chris White)
This pretty song has a medieval air and its courtly sound would, once again, have been in good company on *Odessey And Oracle*. Argent's vocal has a tender, luminous quality that makes this a quietly lovely piece. The imagery of the lyrics is complementary too: 'An orchard… summer senses'. Julia emerges as a kind of anti-'A Rose For Emily' in the flourishing of these phrases.

'If It Don't Work Out' (Rod Argent)
This rousing track is well placed on the collection as the springy piano intro and the staccato strings contrast with 'To Julia's chivalrous arrangement.

'Never My Love' (Dick Adrissi, Don Adrissi)

Written by the Adrissi Brothers and made famous by the wispy version by The Association, of the 'over-easy' MacArthur tracks, this is a favourite, if only for the shiveringly sensual pronunciation of desire in 'You wonder if this heart of mine/Will lose its *desire* for you'! The drums also manage to give just a hint of strength without seeming ridiculous against the frothy melody. This has Madeline Bell, who'd become part of Blue Mink, on backing vocals and was a new sound for Blunstone, as The Zombies had used only male vocals. Blunstone would re-record this with the *New World* line-up and was asked to duet it with Renaissance's Jane Relf, but he turned down the offer.

'It's Not Easy' (Barry Mann, Cynthia Weill)

Boasting Ronny Vernell, the drummer from the Edward Heath Band and the pedigree of Mann/Weill, this seems like it should be a triumph, but Blunstone's usually unmistakable voice borders on the anonymous at times in this arrangement. Finding no lasting success as MacArthur, he allowed the project to run down, but it would not be long before he was coaxed back into the business: this time by White, who offered his and Argent's services as producers. Blunstone was impressed by Argent recordings he'd heard, particularly 'Liar', and readily accepted. Work on *One Year* began quickly after.

'Going To A Go Go' (Marvin Tarplin, Robert Rogers, Warren Moore, William Robinson)

Powered by a hyperactive bass, this live cut from The Zombies shows Blunstone trying out a lower register, and it's a vibrant performance overall. Purists, who feel this one Zombie track proper is the only reason for this collection's inclusion in their catalogue, might feel short-changed. However, the following year saw the release of the compilation *The Zombies And Beyond*, evincing there was still an appetite for the band as it reached 43 on the UK album charts in 2008. With a cover that mimicked *Odessey And Oracle*, it collected Zombies tracks and those of Blunstone and Argent, the band. The Zombies cuts were fairly predictable: 'Time Of The Season', 'She's Not There', 'Tell Her No', 'Summertime', 'Indication', 'I Love You', 'This Will Be Our Year', 'A Rose For Emily' and 'Friends Of Mine'. Blunstone was represented by 'I Don't Believe In Miracles', 'Say You Don't Mind', 'Caroline Goodbye' and 'What Becomes Of The Broken Hearted'. There's also 'Old And Wise', a reflective, almost pastoral song he performed for The Alan Parsons Project's *Eye In The Sky* album in 1982. Written by Parsons and Eric Woolfson, it shares the lovely melancholia that The Zombies also excelled at and is perhaps only marred by the saxophone solo that dates it and can't compete with Blunstone's vocal in terms of pathos. The lyrics have a shade of The Zombies' blend of regret and hope too:

And oh, when I'm old and wise
Bitter words mean little to me

Autumn winds will blow right through me
And someday in the midst of time
When they asked me if I knew you
I'd smile and say you were a friend of mine.

In addition, it followed The Zombies' pattern by being a hit in the US, indeed the first for The Alan Parson's Project, climbing to 21 on the *Billboard* chart.

The Blunstone part of the album shows how he built mostly on the past sound, whereas the Argent cuts are a little broader, including the boogie-woogie of 'Keep On Rolling' and the rockier 'God Gave Rock n Roll to You' and 'Hold Your Head Up', with 'Pleasure' being the most reminiscent of The Zombies' older sound in its trilling piano intro and the cadences of its sweet melody. It also returns to the 'pleasured hands' conceit and crepuscular imagery of 'Time Of The Season':

Lord, that leads the evening hour
Into the night
My love is full of pleasure.

Incidentally, Argent told *Goldmine* about his second band:

Well, they were different players, different ingredients. It sounds very much to me like a crossover. There's a lot of the Zombies feeling on there, to my ears. Personally, I thought the best album Argent ever did was the second album *Ring Of Hands* (the parent album of 'Pleasure'), and I actually prefer that to *All Together Now*, which was the hit album. I actually think that *Ring Of Hands* is sort of undiscovered. I really think that could be re-released and do really well because I think that's a really good album.

It's certainly the one that has the most in common with The Zombies. Returning to this compilation, the later version of the band are represented by 'I Want To Fly' and 'Southside Of The Street'. Despite the span of ages and players, it makes for a coherent album as much as a strong compilation, ascending from the controlled despair of the earlier tracks to the breezy jazz of its final one.

Breathe Out, Breathe In

Personnel
Colin Blunstone: lead vocals except 'Show Me The Way'
Rod Argent: piano, Hammond organ, Wurlitzer electric piano, Mellotron, backing vocals, lead vocal on 'Show Me The Way'
Jim Rodford: bass, backing vocals
Tom Toomey: acoustic and electric guitar
Steve Rodford: drums, percussion, Toontrack Superior Drummer
Recorded: Redhouse Studios
Engineer: Chris Potter
Release Date: 9 May 2011

> But fresher than before ...
> **Ariel, William Shakespeare, *The Tempest***

Receiving the most praise of the latter-day Zombies albums, this is deservedly hailed as a solid and entertaining collection. It has some of The Zombies' hardest rocking tracks as well as some sublimely romantic moments, summed up in the opening and title track that both explore how love makes us look anew at the world. This is developed in the effective cover art, which at first glance looks like an image of space but opens out to reveal a shot of a night-time road with traffic lights streaming like comets. The album has a tenebrous sound overall that looks back to 'Time Of The Season', and Blunstone's voice itself often shimmers like twilight.

Speaking to Terry Staunton in 2011 for *Music Radar*, Blunstone commented on this album: 'I wouldn't say we've tried to copy what went before, but I think playing *Odessey And Oracle* again made a lasting impression on us, how warmly received those concerts were. I think the new album has a flavour to it, an attitude that we had all those years ago'.

Argent concurred, adding:

> Specifically, I think what playing *Odessey And Oracle* did for me was to get me interested in exploring harmonies again, which became part of my brief when we started making the new album... I also wanted all the songs to be reasonably concise, I didn't want them to ramble on, they had to be structured in such a way that they got the job done without overstaying their welcome.

As Far As I Can See had certainly suffered from this, with at least three tracks pushing the five-minute mark.

Another way this album was influenced by their masterpiece is the reappearance of the Mellotron, adding just a little warmth but marrying well to an updated bluesy sound. Blunstone also brought his excellent guitarist Tom Toomey, who played on Blunstone's *The Ghost Of You And Me* in 2009, and who replaces Keith Airey and Mark Johns here, playing both electric and acoustic guitar. Toomey had played previously with Cliff Richard, Jon Anderson and Gene Pitney.

'Breathe Out, Breathe In' (Rod Argent)

Skipping in with a jaunty piano line recalling 'Care Of Cell 44', and also the easy charm of Frank Sinatra's version of 'That's Life', this is an appealing opener. The peals of piano on top of an undulating organ line create a lavish sound, complemented by the lyrics, which recount seeing the beauty of evening with a lover. 'It really is a wonderful sight/As the stars in their millions/Emerge from vermillion/Deepening light'. The arrangement implies a richness of reds.

'Any Other Way' (Colin Blunstone)

One of Blunstone's best compositions, this is a poignant song of regret with an almost humid arrangement that begins a Latin flavour which permeates the album. It's enhanced by a flamenco guitar, with notes falling and gleaming like the raindrops that land as the lovers part. The sudden jolt from the rueful but calm verse to the impatience bursting in the chorus is potent, too. The surge of hope in the melody is countered by a diminished chord that brings it back to a feeling of being resigned. Originally part of Blunstone's impressive *The Ghost Of You And Me* album from 2009, it was accompanied by a dramatic string arrangement that made striking use of pizzicato.

This was the first Zombies song (after the hiatus) to have an official video. Filmed in moody black and white, footage of the band performing the song is interspersed with a storyline depicting how two lovers can never be together. The man is kidnapped and tortured; a few strongly brutal shots of him being tied up and punched are jarring, but it doesn't detract from an achingly romantic song with the simply gorgeous promise: 'And if the world should end today/I'd take my last breath whispering your name/Wondering if you ever felt the same'.

'Play It For Real' (Rod Argent)

This excellent rocker announces itself with a piano riff, which echoes 'Hey Bulldog' from The Beatles' *Yellow Submarine*. It surges from an almost nursery rhyme-esque melody in the verse that recalls Blood Sweat and Tear's 'Spinning Wheel' ever so slightly, to the hardworking chorus with slashing guitar and stabs of organ that evoke their own 'Telescope'. It's a song ultimately of reassurance 'to start anew/The world is waiting and/There's sunshine all the way'. This looks forward to the next track's imagery too – it sounds like they're enjoying themselves immensely.

'Shine On Sunshine' (Rod Argent, Chris White)

Originally recorded by Argent for 1975's *Circus* album, their first after Ballard left, this was a sweet ballad with a hint of Stevie Wonder in the arrangement and in Argent's vocal. But Blunstone elevates it further as he sounds as pure as a morning sunray. It opens and closes with birdsong, and stands out on an album replete with nocturnal motifs, albeit the previous track has prepared us for this.

The melody has a glow of McCartney about it, particularly 'The Long And Winding Road', but hints of the love songs from *McCartney One* also. The middle eight sweeps in seamlessly and is enhanced by some slightly hesitant drums that mimic the imagery of his lover being weary. In fact, Steve Rodford's drumming throughout is a highlight, being simultaneously strong and tender. The choral effect of the Mellotron gives a glint of a gospel sound that hints at this track being an exquisite little prayer.

'Show Me The Way' (Rod Argent)

This opens with a bossa nova beat before slinking down into the bluesy verses. Sung by Argent, he's asking for forgiveness amidst some striking imagery: 'If I bleed/Will you free me?' It's a strong, gritty vocal performance with an effective climbing guitar line in the chorus.

'A Moment In Time' (Rod Argent, Tom Toomey)

There's a Celtic lilt to the melody of this track, co-written by Argent and guitarist Tom Toomey. The acoustic guitars are rich and it's a crisper sound than most Zombies tracks, having a different atmosphere, presumably because of the input of their guitarist. The lyrics discuss the effort to get back on track after hardship and are skillfully matched by the arrangement. In the swaying chorus, with the lines 'Like a rolling cloud/It leaves me blind/Feeling for the breath of angels', the melody sways as the clouds roll in and the line about the breath of angels is extended just that little too long for a shiver of irony. The baroque piano solo builds beautifully but doesn't disturb the elegance of the piece.

There's also a return to 'Brief Candles' in some of the imagery as we're told, 'Life is a stage where/We all just act a part', which paraphrases a metaphor from the same soliloquy from *Macbeth*: 'a poor player that struts and frets his hour upon the stage and is heard no more'. Shakespeare had previously used the analogy in *As You Like It*, but with a less fatalistic intention: 'All the world's a stage/And all the men and women merely players...'. This returns to the themes of time with both its limitations and opportunities.

Overall, the track is one of the best examples of The Zombies' updated sound because it's fresh, but retains the piano flourishes and swirling melody of their earlier tracks. The band made a video to promote this fine song, which included footage of them in the studio.

'Christmas For The Free' (Rod Argent, Chris White)

Appearing as the B-side to another quasi-spiritual song, 'God Gave Rock n Roll to You' in 1973 and the album *In Deep*, Rod Argent told Terry Staunton about this re-recording: 'It's close to the original, but more polished now. I think it suffered from being put together in a hurry in its first incarnation'.

The Argent version is more understated, with a lighter backing that actually works better. For some reason, the stop-start piano in the verse here grates; naturally, Blunstone's vocal is excellent.

'Another Day' (Rod Argent)
Probably the most dated track on the album, the drums and guitar have a 1980s stadium rock vibe, whilst the melody and arrangement recalls The Alan Parson's Project. However, the rhythmic shifts attract attention and the organ is very 'Time Of The Season'.

'I Do Believe' (Rod Argent)
Blessed with a superb keyboard solo that has submerged notes bubbling and roiling, this would have made for a more accomplished and memorable final track. It's also the longest on the album, with the lyrics rounding up the motifs of urban night-time:

> There's a thrill in the evening
> With the sun going down
> And I can't help believing
> Something good that I've found
> There's a note from the city
> Hanging hard in the air.

The idea of regeneration and a link back to the opening track can be found in the penultimate verse: 'Like a baby I'm learning to breathe'.

'Let It Go' (Rod Argent)
An engaging ballad, it's not the strongest track and is fine on its own, but here, allows the album to deflate. In its favour, there is the hymn-like organ lending it a gravitas, the shimmering chorus that Blunstone and Argent sing together and the hints of gospel found elsewhere on the album are resolved here. Telling the story of a love soured, the lyrics reveal, 'I long to see you/ Back again/In sunshine after/Summer rain'. This returns to one of the central images of 'If There Were Any Other Way', but now the lovers didn't part: they stayed together and made each other miserable! It's a dour closing to an otherwise warm album.

Conclusion
Probably the most successful of The Zombies' later albums, *Breathe Out, Breathe In* is accomplished and assured. Released in the 50th anniversary year of The Zombies' first rehearsal together, it's a testament to not only their longevity but also their ability to reinvent without losing sight of what

makes them The Zombies. Argent told Dave Thompson for *Goldmine* in 2011: 'I think it's a terrific collection of material. It's got a lot of resonance. We haven't tried to go back to early Zombies because it isn't. But it's got loads of harmonies on it, and it's a real band album'.

Still Got That Hunger

Personnel
Colin Blunstone: lead vocals
Rod Argent: keyboards, backing and lead vocals
Tom Toomey: guitar, backing vocals
Jim Rodford: bass, backing vocals
Steve Rodford: drums,
Producer: Christopher Marc Potter
Recorded: State of the Ark Studios, The Potting Shed
Release Date: 9 October 2015
Chart placings: US: 24 (*Billboard* Independent Albums)

> Let us not burthen our remembrance with
> A heaviness that's gone
> **Prospero, William Shakespeare, *The Tempest***

With artwork by Terry Quirk, this is an album looking back over its shoulder in many ways but is also about exploring what the future still has to offer. Bringing the band squarely into 2015, they raised money for the album through PledgeMusic, although this was mostly a ruse to garner publicity rather than because of a real financial need.

There was also a change in production, as Chris Potter, producer of The Verve's *Urban Hymns*, was at the helm. Argent told Jim Sullivan for *Cape Cod Time* in 2015:

> We wanted very much to try and go back to a way of recording that we used to have with four tracks. You'd record with the whole band in one room and work off each other, making music the old way when everyone was listening and responding to everything. And we missed that. We thought if we could find a really good vintage studio, one with a great Steinway piano, we would love to go back to that way of recording. To do that, you have to have a really good producer because you have to stay in there and work on the ambience and what you're hearing. You can't keep interrupting right in that moment. Strangely enough, we got a phone call from Chris Potter, who said he'd seen some YouTube footage of us playing at Central Park and he loved it and said, 'I'd love to produce an album for you'.

Similar to how they prepared for *Odessey And Oracle*, the band thoroughly rehearsed the tracks before they went into the studio, where the songs were mostly recorded live. Blunstone told Bob Ruggiero for *Houston Press* on 26 April 2017 that many of the vocals he'd laid down were as a guide, but on listening back, they decided to keep them. Not only did this create a fresh atmosphere on the album, it also meant that tracks would be ready to go out on the road. Jim Rodford was particularly keen to play live and told *Times*

Series that this line-up was the best band he'd ever worked with, including his stint with The Kinks.

'Moving On' (Rod Argent)

This is a bluesy, guitar-driven opener that has a dirtier sound than previous Zombies' tracks. In fact, it's a re-writing of the instrumental 'Moving On' (sometimes billed as 'Movin' On', but not on the label of the LP) included on the saxophonist Barbara Thompson's collaboration with Argent – *Ghosts* from 1982. The tempo there is more of a shuffle and the melody is carried by a synth, whilst this version has a rootsier sound.

Blunstone's gleaming vocal works well against this backing, not being dimmed even by the razoring guitar lines that cut across. The vocals, shared with Argent in the middle eight, have the same richness as their older harmonies and the split guitar/organ solo also harks back. Blunstone commented to Jason Barnard for *The Strangebrew* in 2015 that this was one of his favourite songs on the album, being a great track to play live.

Lyrically, this is a song preoccupied with leaving the past behind (it has something in common with 'I Must Move'); it's a curious choice to open their most nostalgic album. The official video is black and white footage of the current line-up performing the song to an appreciative crowd, waving their *Zombie Heaven* box sets, enhancing an ironic retrospection. Returning to the lyrics, the syntax is strained at times, e.g. 'In my life no more grief and no sorrow/Won't allow darkness my life to define'. Nevertheless, the song evinces how the band's signatures – Blunstone's pure tone and Argent's keyboard virtuosity – are timeless. A live version recorded for the radio station WFUV is also a treat; stripped back to just piano and vocals, it shows the power of the driving melody.

'Chasing The Past' (Rod Argent)

Rob Sheffield, reviewing the album for *Rolling Stone,* said this song sounded most like the 1960s incarnation of the band 'where they're hung up on a dream of yesterday, yet still aiming to "take tomorrow and give it hell"'. In some respects, this description could apply to the album as a whole, but it's particularly apt here. Continuing the strong start to this collection, it also references the title, asserting that the singer has the hunger to conquer the future. Characterised by pretty arpeggios that ripple behind Blunstone's strong but tender vocal, it's a moving song. The swirling organ solo is a highlight, as is the simultaneously regretful and triumphant timbre of Tom Toomey's excellent guitar lines.

'Edge Of The Rainbow' (Rod Argent)

This returns to the rainbow imagery that opening track 'Moving On' established, but also changes the mood with some honky tonk piano and a strolling blues riff, capped by another rich Blunstone vocal. An uncomplicated lyric, it reminds us of how bad times get better. Blunstone told Jason Barnard: 'Rod wrote the melody with my voice in mind. I've got quite a good range, so it gives me a chance to really go for some top notes. It's a good song for me to sing'. It would be added to their 2019 sets on the same bill as Brian Wilson.

'New York' (Argent)

When The Zombies first arrived in New York, they likened it to *The Naked City*. White and Grundy had even been on the scene when a man was gunned down. Argent, too, felt an initial hostility, telling Bob Lefsetz: 'When I first went to New York, I hated it. It was so full of energy and aggression ... But, in fact, it became one of my favourite cities because it seemed to have an honesty about it...'. This paraphrases the second verse of this song, which pays tribute to a city that saw The Zombies achieve real acclaim and gave them the gift of touring with their heroes. The song begins with a general tribute to America and name-checks Elvis, Miles Davies, Jerry Lee Lewis and Ray Charles, before relocating to New York itself and recounting the events of the Murray the K gigs that the band took part in, with them giving thanks: 'helped us join the party/With our English Rock and Roll'. It gave The Zombies an insight into the American music scene that not all British bands had, and they were often aware of soon-to-be classics before the UK had heard of them. This is how they came to be interested in recording Smokey Robinson and Donald White's 'My Girl', but were ultimately deterred when it slipped into the British charts ahead of them.

Whilst a sweet tribute in one way, in another, this is one of the most dated songs, with its 1980s style drums and an atmosphere of Boston (band, not place!) about it. Being the longest track on the album, its slight melody doesn't hold the attention enough either.

'I Want You Back Again' (Rod Argent)

A remake that is undoubtedly superior to the original, the album is worth hearing for this alone. Slightly slower, with more of a shuffle and a hint of discordant piano in the chorus, it's a tense but alluring sound, much more likely to have the lover return than the first version. The piano solo has flickers of Mike Garson with flashes of Gershwin, and the crescendo at its climax is a chilly thrill, owing a debt to Tom Petty's live version. The snarling guitar adds power, creating an uneasy conflict between the yearning lyric and the immediacy of the arrangement. Argent told Jason Barnard for *Strangebrew*:

> We came across a version a couple of years ago by Tom Petty and he recorded it on a live album. We thought, 'this is really good, why aren't we doing this?', and we started to do it and we stayed very true to the original character of the song. But because we were playing it night after night and really enjoying it, it started to seat itself in the way that we really, really liked

and we thought we've got to record this for posterity, so it became the only old piece of material on the album. As you know, everything else is newly composed, but that was one we really, really enjoy doing. We did it live, absolutely live, and it took us about 20 minutes to record. I loved the way that I could actually use a real acoustic piano, which, of course, we didn't use the first time – we used electric piano – and the possibilities that gave me on the record. We use a sampled piano on stage and we love playing it on stage still, but it was just a way of combining what we wanted to do with a piece of old material and just taking it one step further. It was a real joy to do it.

It's a joy to listen to also.

'And We Were Young Again' (Rod Argent, Catherine Argent)

Using a Zombies/Argent tic – beginning a sentence with 'and' – this heart-warming track has an unusual songwriting credit, as Catherine is Argent's wife. Cathy leaves notes for Argent in his luggage when he's touring and some of the lyrics were taken from these. It sustains the nostalgic tone of the album and has the beautiful line, 'you took my hand as if I were precious'. However, the arrangement is less successful than most on the album, with the jarring guitar tone and the keyboards sounding too MOR (middle of the road). One wonders how a simple piano backing and Blunstone's velvet vocal would have illuminated the latent sensuality here.

'Maybe Tomorrow' (Rod Argent)

A *Flaming Pie* flavour is captured on this up-tempo track, and coincidentally, *Flaming Pie* was also a nostalgic reference to a legend about how The Beatles acquired their name, and McCartney's influence is here in more ways than one: a snippet of the lyric of 'Yesterday' is used to conclude a song about hoping for a reconciliation.

Argent told the *Strangebrew* podcast:

I thought it would be an affectionate nod in the direction of The Beatles, just at the very end, to get Colin to sing, just like The Beatles used to say (Rod sings) 'I believe in yesterday' and it was just like an amusing little aside really. We got a message just before the album came out, from Sony, who said, 'You can't put this album out; we're blocking it, because you're quoting from The Beatles', and we were absolutely distraught and, as a last resort, our management company in America got in touch with Paul McCartney's personal manager, whom they didn't know, and said 'I don't know if there's anything you can do but this is supposed to be released in three or four days' time and I know it's a lot to ask, but I just wonder if there is any way you could override this?' We got a phone call two days later saying Paul McCartney has downloaded this, he thinks it's great and said, 'Just go ahead' as he'd personally given the approval. So that was a really lovely little story and, we thought, what a star.

The dancing piano lines provide the musical optimism with Blunstone's vocal light but assured.

'Now I Know I'll Never Get Over You' (Colin Blunstone)
This first appeared on Blunstone's *The Ghost Of You And Me*. It's a serviceable ballad with some glowing guitar lines, but the melody and the over-crowded lyrics don't really fit. Argent adds a typically glorious keyboard solo, but again, it doesn't match and the track stands out as not really fitting in with the others. The original version works better with its determined but elegant string arrangement.

'Little One' (Rod Argent)
This is a reworking of 'Little Girl', an originally instrumental track that Argent wrote for Barbara Thompson's *Ghost*. It's a simple bluesy track with vocal and keyboard and proves how well Blunstone and Argent work together or as 'sweet as a symphony'.

'Beyond The Borderline' (Rod Argent)
Covering similar ground as other tracks, e.g. passing through into a better time and place, this is an upbeat closing to the album, with Blunstone and Argent harmonising delightfully together and Argent taking the lead on the middle eight – it's gently triumphant. And not only did *Still Got That Hunger* make it into the *Billboard* chart, but it also caused *Odessey and Oracle* to enter the chart, too.

Conclusion
Rolling Stone gave the album a short if warm review, remarking that 'Chasing The Past' sounded most like The Zombies of old and noted that they now produced a more 'straightforward blues-rock sound'.

Argent was delighted, telling *Strangebrew*:

We got a call from *Billboard* magazine, and they said, 'Do you realise for the first time in 50 years as The Zombies, you are actually in six *Billboard* charts, but the album has made the top hundred album sales?', which was absolutely fantastic and, you know, we were hoping for some sort of reaction to the album but, you know, to actually make that chart was fantastic, so it does feel very exciting actually.

2015 was a strong year for the band, with them performing on 1960s nostalgia cruises alongside The Moody Blues and then appearing at Glastonbury playing the Avalon tent on the Sunday. Curiously, Stephen

Hawking was also on the bill that year and was a fellow alumnus of St Albans School... Argent explained to Chris Harvey of *The Independent* in 2023:

When we did Glastonbury a few years ago, we were in one of the smaller arenas. It was a marquee, and I guess it must have held up to 5,000 people, but when we started the set, there were just a few people in there, and I thought, 'Oh God, I hope this is not going to be embarrassing'. But when we started playing, it filled up, mostly with young people. And when we did 'Time Of The Season', this huge audience of young people went completely crazy. And I said to Colin afterwards, 'How do they know it? It's never been a hit here'.

Different Game

Personnel
Colin Blunstone: lead vocals
Rod Argent: keyboards, backing and lead vocal on 'Dropped Reeling And Stupid', Steinway piano, Rhodes Stage 73 electric piano, Wurlitzer electric piano, Mellotron, harmonica
Tom Toomey: guitar, backing vocals
Soren Koch: bass, backing vocals
Steve Rodford: drums, percussion
Q Strings:
Laura Strasford: first violin
Ellie Stanford: second violin
Amy Stanford: viola
Jess Cox: cello
Producer: Rod Argent and Dale Hanson
Engineer: Dale Hanson and Steve Orchard
Release date: 21 March 2023
Chart placings: UK: did not chart, US: did not chart

What's past is prologue
Antonio, William Shakespeare, *The Tempest*

After several attempts (four to be exact!), The Zombies were finally inducted into The Rock 'n' Roll Hall Of Fame on 29 March 2019 – 50 years to the day that 'Time Of The Season' ascended to the top spot in the US. Susanna Hoffs gave a speech in praise of their 'elegance, soulfulness' and 'foggy London intrigue', and how it 'was love at first listen' for her. And for many others, it seems, exemplified by the rapturous response to the songs they performed live that evening: 'Time Of The Season', 'Tell Her No', 'This Will Be Our Year' and 'She's Not There', with White and Grundy also back in the band. They then joined Def Leppard for their encore of 'All The Young Dudes'.

Not long after, the quartet played as part of a bill that starred Brian Wilson – 'Something Great from '68'. The Zombies played a split set: the first half included their singles and some new tracks, including 'Merry-Go-Round'. The second half was a full performance of *Odessey And Oracle*. However, the next time The Zombies toured, in 2021, White and Grundy had returned to their own projects. The touring Zombies band also had to undergo a sad change: just days after returning from gigging in Florida in 2018, Jim Rodford fell down the stairs and died aged 76. Dave Davies posted on Twitter that he was too upset to articulate his feelings about Rodford but commented: 'I always thought Jim would live forever in true rock 'n' roll fashion'. Argent called him his 'dear cousin and lifelong friend' and noted how he 'was unfailingly committed to local music'. His loss was felt keenly at the Induction, too, with Argent's heartfelt thanks to Rodford being a particularly poignant moment.

The touring band now consisted of Steve Rodford, Tom Toomey and new bassist Soren Koch. It was this line-up that joined Argent and Blunstone for their most current album, *Different Game* in 2023.

Different Game saw The Zombies victorious, with *The Telegraph*'s Andrew Perry proclaiming: 'Stylistically, *Different Game* runs an extraordinary gamut, at one point flipping in a heartbeat from 'I Want To Fly's consummate chamber-pop, composed only of elaborate classical strings and voice, to 'Got To Move On's driving, Spencer Davis Group-style R&B'. It's an apposite description that sums up the tones of the album well; indeed, this could be applied to the other later Zombies albums, too. *The Watford Observer* also commented on the album, calling the band 'legendary' and providing a pleasing circularity since its reporting on The Herts Beat competition in 1964. In fact, *Different Game* was well received across the board, with nearly every reviewer remarking on the extraordinary vocal talents of Blunstone and Argent's seemingly effortless virtuosity. For anyone who'd really been listening to all of the 'latter-day' Zombies albums, this was more than old news... but *Different Game* isn't just a testament to Argent and Blunstone – it's the sound of a band working joyously together.

Interviewing both Blunstone and Argent about the release of their latest album in February 2023, Argent explained the genesis of it:

> We were coming off a year where we'd pretty much been in the States. And this incarnation of the band, which has been going since 1999 or early 2000, sounded better than it ever had to me. It was just so exciting. Our career in America was extraordinary – in the last ten years, it's really had a complete upward curve. When we first went over in the early 2000s, I remember playing in Georgia and having 12 people in the audience and thinking, oh my goodness... If we play now, we might have 2000 people. It ended just before COVID, that period of playing, with being inducted into the Rock 'n' Roll Hall Of Fame. And we couldn't wait to start recording a new album. I'd just written two songs at that point. We recorded them in a way I was keen to record – with us all being in the studio at the same time, with me producing and Dale Hanson, our wonderful sound engineer. We wanted to capture that feeling – of a band bouncing off each other, responding to Colin's guide vocal.

The Zombies had planned to record prior to the COVID crisis occurring, and whilst this resulted in a delay for its recording, particularly as Koch lives in Denmark, Argent saw it as a strange blessing: 'I'd never had that luxury before, being unstressed and unconcerned about having to do other things. Like, start writing a song, getting excited about it, but then losing my way. That was an unlooked-for advantage'.

At least four tracks were played live prior to being recorded and I asked Blunstone how they were received: 'They've all gone down extraordinarily well. It's a bit of an art incorporating brand-new material with classic rock songs that were written and recorded 50 and 60 years ago. It's quite bizarre, really, but it seems to work with the Zombies. We're really fortunate in that respect'.

I wondered how they kept an authentic Zombies sound and Blunstone explained:

> The Zombies, right from the beginning, were a keyboard-based band at a time when that was very unusual in the time of The Shadows and The Ventures. We're a keyboard-based band that features three-part harmonies... we've always done that and that's one of the links that will take you to Zombies based music. Also, we were all very interested in a very wide spectrum of music... that has always been a strength, but it can be a bit of a weakness because people in the industry love to categorise and we've always been a bit difficult to categorise. The final thing I'd say is the dominant writer has always been Rod and the lead singer has always been me and that's very much a link back to 1964. There's a lot that links this album back.

'Different Game' (Argent)

A brooding ballad with an atmosphere of Procol Harum (and, of course, Argent favourite, Bach) in the organ sound, this has Blunstone taking the lead vocal and Argent prominent on backing vocals – both of them poignantly sing the opening line. It's a reflective song looking back on a simpler time when 'life seemed such a different game'. Argent told Chris Harvey for *The Independent* in 2023 how an unnamed rock singer inspired it: 'I was struck by the fact that as he got older, he couldn't come to terms with how different he was feeling about things. And he started blaming all his bandmates around him'. It broke up the band, he says, and it struck him as a universal theme: how 'as you age, you look back – and the bitterness and regret that you can sometimes feel. But you can't blame other people for it'.

Whilst the retrospective lyrics might make this seem like a pertinent opener, it may well have been potent as the final track, or at least a later one: the understated strings bestow a wistful tone and the final part of the track is an extended coda of only strings, sounding almost like an elegy. Nevertheless, it ends on an unresolved chord, leaving us with the feeling that there is, of course, still more to come. Q Strings are the quartet performing here, comprised of three violinists, who are sisters, and a cellist, and their dignified but powerful playing is a highlight of the album.

'Dropped Reeling & Stupid' (Argent)

Perhaps this would have been the sharper opening track, as it's a cool blues with a strong Blunstone vocal that belies his age. Ignited by the band's tour bus breaking down in the Arizona desert, Argent took inspiration both lyrically (using the idea of desertion as a metaphor for being jilted by a lover) and for the album cover, as he took a photograph of the tour bus being towed away. Released as the first single, the accompanying animated video riffed on this too. Blunstone elaborated to *Rolling Stone*:

> We were travelling from Southern California to Tucson when our tour van's engine suddenly caught fire! We spent about five hours stranded in the remote Arizona desert, but thanks to our intrepid team and crew, we were rescued and made it to our next show! It was a harrowing experience, but also beautiful and surreal.

'Rediscover' (Argent)
This track incorporates 11th and 13th chords and Argent explained how these had been an influence since the very early days of the band. 'I got that from listening to a beautiful Keith Jarrett version of 'When I Fall In Love'. The second chord he played was a B flat to another voicing of the chord and I just loved it'. It opens with a dreamy acapella refrain, glowing with warm harmonies, before hesitant drums and a strolling piano line lead us to the singer's rediscovery of love. This song celebrates finding freedom in a way that 'I Want to Fly' strives for, enhanced by a carefree 1950s doo-wop vibe provided by the celestial backing vocals. Blunstone's voice simply caresses the melody here. Whilst this album doesn't exhibit much of a shift in their style or sound, this is a track that shows them trying something new, as this is an area of 1950s music they haven't previously explored.

'Runaway' (Argent)
One of the first new songs to be recorded, this is a creeping blues enlivened by some intriguing and jazzy chords. It recalls 'Show Me The Way' from *Breathe Out, Breathe In* and explores a similar type of romantic confusion, as in 'How can you make me feel my love was such a crime?'

'You Could Be My Love' (Argent)
Unrelentingly romantic, this ballad has Argent's piano rippling like starlight on water and showcases a silky vocal from Blunstone, illustrating the strength of their partnership. Whilst this incarnation of The Zombies have undoubtedly cohered well, this track reminds one of the band's original magic in the pairing of Blunstone's vocal and Argent's keyboards.

'Merry-Go-Round' (Argent)
This optimistic track ('Once there was wasteland...now there's graceland') was the first song from the album that the band played live and one of the earliest to be recorded. Argent commented: 'There's always a young component when we play in the audience. For instance, we play 'Time Of The Season' and it goes down a complete storm, and then we play 'Merry-

Go-Round' immediately afterwards and it goes down almost as well. That is just so rejuvenating'. This probably explains why The Zombies' 2023 tour is named after a line in the song: Life is a Merry-Go-Round. It was also released with a video showing the band playing live and being adored by some very appreciative fans. It's easy to see how it makes for an exciting live performance and the false ending adds to this, too.

The track evokes 'Play It For Real' from *Breathe Out, Breathe In,* as they're both driven by a pounding piano riff that's fortified by some snaking guitar licks. The lyrics are similar too, with the analogy of life being a game alluded to in both. Of course, the title track of this album also uses this metaphor.

'Love You While I Can' (Argent)
Released on Valentine's Day as the second single off the album, this is reminiscent of early Chris White tracks in its delicacy. A twinkling guitar line characterises a sweet little love song and Blunstone is genuinely breathy here, further softened by the tender backing vocals. Susanna Hoffs commented that there 'aren't enough adjectives' to describe his vocals...

'I Want to Fly' (Argent)
I asked Argent why he'd decided to revisit this track, which was firstly part of *As Far as I Can See* from 2009:

> I always thought Colin with Chris Gunning was a very, very special artistic partnership. When we did 'I Want To Fly', I did the original string arrangement. I didn't think it was bad, but when we were redoing this album, and we were in charge of the process ourselves, I knew Colin had a particular affection for this song. I said it would be wonderful to revisit that experience of *One Year* with Chris Gunning doing a beautiful arrangement.

Sadly, Gunning died aged 78, a month after the album's release.

When Argent invited Gunning to work on the track, he wouldn't let Gunning hear his own arrangement beforehand, telling him: 'I want your totally pristine response to the song'. This strategy must have worked because Argent was delighted with Gunning's work. He continued:

> We absolutely love the result. It's a real return to some of the feelings I had when I heard *One Year*. Some of Chris White's songs – 'Her Song', the marriage of Colin's voice and Chris Gunning's arrangement is very magical. I think we've caught some of that. It wasn't an attempt to say we haven't got a song. It was one we both felt like an occasional thing to revisit and record in a truer way.

Previously, Blunstone had remarked to Jason Barnard for *Strangebrew* in 2015: 'I love that song. I'm always asking Rod to put it into the set. I really don't understand his reluctance to do it. But I think it's a very special song'. Argent must have listened in the end ...

This version has a more portentous and muscular string arrangement with no piano at all, and a poignant but strong vocal from Blunstone that rivals the one he recorded over 15 years ago. The longer pauses, at times, reflect better the latent struggle in the lyrics and it seems a very generous act for Argent to remove himself from this version, giving his 'old mucker' the pure limelight – an exquisite work all round and a fine tribute to Gunning.

'Got To Move On' (Argent)

A winning mid-tempo rocker that sees Argent return to the first instrument he learnt to play: the harmonica. The swinging drum pattern at the start looks back to Grundy's style and the image of falling tears is mirrored in the dripping piano notes. The whole keyboard line, in fact, is sardonic and complemented by Blunstone's coolly resigned vocal. The guitar solo is jittery but controlled and it's a solid band performance all round. There's a vitality to many of the tracks, resulting from the majority of them being recorded in around four hours. It's probably the track that sounds most like we'd expect a 21st-century Zombie to sound! Argent explained to me: 'We're doing this [recording new music] primarily so that we've got a way to bring things that still excite us. It's the same process as when we were 16 years old'.

'The Sun Will Rise Again' (Blunstone)

Argent described this Blunstone composition, which originally graced *The Ghost Of Me And You* in 2009, as 'beautiful'. He's right. Partly written for Blunstone's daughter, this is a plaintive but simultaneously optimistic track, asking, 'How can you love if you've never tasted tears?' and includes the bittersweet observation:

Love has its price
And everyone must pay
Just as I must set you free
Watch you fly away

Blunstone told me: 'Rod suggested it out of the blue. We've turned it around in the opposite way. Tom Toomey is mirroring what I play on guitar normally. We've done the reverse on this song (removed strings). I think Rod quite liked the idea of having an acoustic, mystical song at the end of the album'. Argent added:

I absolutely loved the song when I heard it. A beautiful guitar arrangement. I always used to love the way that The Beatles would sometimes end an album with a lovely thought to leave you with, an intimate thought – the love you take is equal to the love you make. Just a little thought to go out on. The sun will rise again will be a beautiful thought to leave the album on. We initially thought of doing it with just voice and guitar, but we expanded it a little bit.

Toomey had the difficult task of replacing the original piano with his guitar note for note and did so with painstaking skill that allows the fragile melody to fly. Blunstone's vocal is at times almost conversational and, at others, as if he's singing a lullaby, or looking back to 'Summertime', directed towards a child. Argent's glowing keyboard comes in halfway through like sunrays through clouds and it is a moment of gentle beauty. The 2009 version is also an excellent interpretation, with almost cautionary strings that remind of the French Romantic movement, in particular, Berlioz. However, this version showcases the fine songwriting prowess of Blunstone. A pity, then, that some reviewers singled this track out as a superior Argent composition!

Conclusion
Different Game is not really different in terms of The Zombies' sound or of Argent's songwriting, but is more the pinnacle of their perfecting their later, blues-rock tone, established on *Breathe Out, Breathe In*. When I spoke to them via Zoom, both were obviously excited by their music, old and new, yet seemed genuinely surprised to mean so much to so many. Over 60 years of supreme vocals, flawless keyboard playing and songs that exhibit sheer joy in their existence really cannot be underestimated.

The release of the 2023 documentary *Hung Up On A Dream*, directed by Robert Schwartzman, continues The Zombies' afterlife and further highlights their relevance all these years later.

Live And Compilations Round-Up

And when I have required some heavenly music...
Prospero, William Shakespeare, *The Tempest*

Live At The BBC (2003)

This replicates the final disc from *Zombie Heaven – (Disc 4: Live On The
BBC)*. *Uncut* commented in their 2004 review: 'Proving conclusively that
white boys from Watford in polo-necks and glasses could acquit themselves
more than adequately in the R&B department, The Zombies were arguably
the most underrated UK group of the 1960s'. The album was released again as
The BBC Radio Sessions but also includes The Four Tops' 1966 US hit 'Loving
You Is Sweeter Than Ever' (written by Ivy Jo Hunter and Stevie Wonder).

Live At The Bloomsbury Theatre, London (2005)

'Andorra' is a welcome opener, being a compelling song and a great bridge
between The Zombies and their solo odysseys. However, it's sped up and
misses the atmosphere of the original. Despite this, the sparing organ solo
is a different take on the dry, blustery Spanish guitar on Blunstone's version
and it's well worth hearing. 'What Becomes Of The Broken Hearted' is
enhanced by the addition of a striking opening riff that is returned to in
the middle before a whizzy little solo from Argent. There are also winning
versions of 'Mystified' and 'Sanctuary' from *Out Of The Shadows*, which give
a neglected area of their back catalogue a new sheen. The obvious Argent
cuts are joined by an elegant version of 'Pleasure' from *Ring Of Hands* and
Blunstone's shiningly assured tone adds to the song. 'Say You Don't Mind'
is utterly captivating and rapturously received and is followed by an equally
tender 'Misty Roses'. Written by Tim Hardin for his debut album in 1966,
it was covered by many, including Cilla Black, Peggy Lee, Sonny and Cher
and Bobby Darin, but none have the perfect gossamer tones of Blunstone.
Hardin's cut is short, gentle and based around 7th chords, but Blunstone
puts a jazzy inflection on it with the use of 13ths that hold the melody off
from being too nebulous or misty. In a dialogue with myself, Argent recalled
the original recording: 'We asked Chris Gunning [responsible for the elegant
arrangements on *One Year*] to do something very adventurous. It was my idea
to go into a strong, very Avant-garde way of approaching the song. I said it
would be great if you let it develop in a Bela Bartok way'. It's a moment of
unparalleled beauty on this album, too.

The *Odessey* tracks are buoyant if occasionally swamped by the longer
numbers; it was a wise decision to perform the album in its entirety for the
40th anniversary. Whilst 'Indication' should be a sparky moment, it's one
of few tracks where Blunstone seems unsure and the wash of sound on
the 45 is lacking here, which might explain why it doesn't appear on other
live collections. However, it is enlivened by a thread of 'God Rest Ye Merry

Gentlemen' in the organ solo, showing that this really could be a thing of power. The carol uses the Aeolian mode and Argent had been inspired by Miles Davies, right at the start of his career because of his use of this. To be completely honest, some of The Zombies' tracks here aren't as punchy as the solo ones. Even 'She's Not There' loses its grandeur under heavy organ work, a wailing guitar solo, and then a twist of 'Day Tripper'. Yet, there are live collections where these begin to blossom. As a two-disc collection, it's an outstanding overview of their career and evidence of the technical expertise in their line-up at the time.

Odessey And Oracle: 40th Anniversary Live Concert (2008)

Even if the singles had garnered the success they were owed, it would have been challenging for the band to tour much of *Odessey And Oracle* because of difficulties with the Mellotron. Forty years later, advances in technology meant that the whole album could be re-created with a high degree of fidelity. Darian Sahanaja, keyboardist with The Wondermints, played Mellotron, with Argent admitting that he knew the album better than he did! Accompanied by a DVD that touchingly makes the pride of the band apparent, the first half is the entire album, sumptuously and authentically brought to life, with the second half including obvious Zombies, Argent and Blunstone hits, but the lesser performed 'Her Song' from *One Year* is also included.

In *The Sunday Times*, Robert Sandall wrote: 'Still more niche in their appeal to the heritage concert crowd are The Zombies, a British band from the 1960s who have just re-formed to perform their second album *Odessey And Oracle*. Many of us were barely aware of the existence of this psychedelic pop classic'. This is overstating the obscurity, as the mid-nineties had seen *Odessey And Oracle* moving into the second half of 100 best lists, but nevertheless, the point was made that an album, which had initially failed to chart, could draw a crowd.

Being painstaking in their recreation of the sound, Blunstone was particularly impressed by White, saying to Rich Bennett: 'I really do admire Chris White though, because from 1967 to 2008, he hadn't picked up a bass guitar, and he played it note perfectly'.

Live In Concert At Metropolis Studios (2012)

Accompanied by a DVD that shows how intimate this gig was, it captures 19 songs, most of which are predictable but welcome favourites, but 'If There Was Any Other Way' and 'Whenever You're Ready' are great additions. 'I Don't Believe in Miracles' from Blunstone's *Ennismore* is also strong. Coincidentally, Hot Chocolate, whom Ballard would write 'You Win Again' for, did record a song declaring 'You Sexy Thing (I Believe In Miracles)'. White told Russo:

> Russ wrote a great song for the album that should have been a hit. Russ thought it should have been titled 'I Do Believe In Miracles'. He thought

the negativity of it stopped it from being more successful. One of the things that hurt his (Colin's) song in England was that Colin played it live with his touring band for the first time on a radio show, and radio stations kept playing that version instead of the studio version because there was a limitation on how many records you could play on the radio. The live version was totally different from the record, which is why it never sold.

Ballard said to Henry Yates at *Classic Rock* regarding 'God Gave Rock 'n' Roll To You':

It was wonderful to feel myself come out of that depression. I felt so 'up'. It probably only took 20 minutes to write it. I'd always liked gospel. With the lyric, I was saying that we live on this incredible planet, and when you find a passion, this world makes sense. Whereas, if you settle for a job to pay the bills, it's very sad.

'Say You Don't Mind' is performed too and had been part of The Zombies' late 1960s live set, with Blunstone suggesting that they record it. Whilst this was not to be, Blunstone himself did, of course, record the track and it closes his debut album *One Year*. Written by original Moody Blue Denny Laine, it was first orchestrated by John Paul Jones but never made the charts. Blunstone's gorgeously grieving vocal owns it, whether on *One Year* or the live version here. And he was able to sing the song in the same key, being disciplined enough to use a vocal coach and to do regular exercises.

Live In The UK (2013)
This is a short but strong collection and 'Breathe Out, Breathe In' is a welcome addition to the setlist.

The Decca Stereo Anthology (2002)
This has a place in the collection, but these versions don't surpass the mono mixes. However, the travesty of having a 'She's Not There' lacking the overdubbed drums is rectified as Hugh Grundy re-recorded this in 2002 using his original snare, and for this alone, the collection is valuable. He also took the opportunity to restore tambourine to the mix of 'Is This the Dream?' The anthology undoes the damage from the hastily mixed stereo versions on *The World Of The Zombies* cheapo set.

Afterword

Considering longevity, Argent told Jim Sullivan in 2015:

I always remember thinking at the time, we were still idolising people like Muddy Waters and John Lee Hooker, who seemed ancient to us at the time and they were in their 40s or 50s. We had no problem with that at all. We were looking at an art form that was a source of rock 'n' roll and what rock 'n' roll had led from, the various beginnings, including those. I thought if rock 'n' roll grows up, we may feel different about it and that's entirely how I feel now. Really young people are coming to us and loving what we do and that's fantastic.

Whilst Argent and Blunstone are still recording and touring with The Zombies, of course, White has developed The Chris White Experience – a project that has seen five volumes of mostly previously unreleased tracks collected. The list of his collaborators on these songs is a testament to the esteem in which he's held: Mark Knopfler, Matthew Fisher and Stuart Elliot, amongst them. Grundy has continued a musical career, playing with Joe Public (not the New York combo who sang 'Live And Learn') and being a publican himself. Before his sadly early death in 2004, Atkinson had been a giant of A&R, and had received the President's Merit Award for his work.

In White's acceptance speech from 2019, as the band were inducted into the Rock 'n' Roll Hall Of Fame, he explained: 'Music and songs are the bookmarks in all our lives; it's the language that binds us all together...' The Zombies have added beautifully to this lexicon.

When Kay Halle, friend of George Gershwin, first heard 'Summertime', she said she knew it would be beloved by the world. I felt almost the same when first hearing *Odessey And Oracle*: that it would *continue* to be beloved by the world ...

Would you like to write for Sonicbond Publishing?

At Sonicbond Publishing we are always on the look-out for authors, particularly for our two main series:

On Track. Mixing fact with in depth analysis, the On Track series examines the work of a particular musical artist or group. All genres are considered from easy listening and jazz to 60s soul to 90s pop, via rock and metal.

On Screen. This series looks at the world of film and television. Subjects considered include directors, actors and writers, as well as entire television and film series. As with the On Track series, we balance fact with analysis.

While professional writing experience would, of course, be an advantage the most important qualification is to have real enthusiasm and knowledge of your subject. First-time authors are welcomed, but the ability to write well in English is essential.

Sonicbond Publishing has distribution throughout Europe and North America, and all books are also published in E-book form. Authors will be paid a royalty based on sales of their book.

Further details are available from www.sonicbondpublishing.co.uk. To contact us, complete the contact form there or
email info@sonicbondpublishing.co.uk